Right with God

Right with God

John Blanchard

MOODY PRESS
CHICAGO

Moody Paperback Edition, 1978

The use of selected references from various versions of the Bible in this publication does not necessarily imply publisher endorsement of the versions in their entirety.

Library of Congress Cataloging in Publication Data
Blanchard, John, 1932-
    Right with God.

    1. Apologetics—20th century. I. Title.
BT1102.B53   1978   248'.4   78-6809
ISNB 0-8024-7357-1

Printed in the United States of America

Contents

Introduction

They were typical modern teenagers, enjoying themselves at a Somerset youth club. The place had been alive with movement and music, but now the record player was switched off and the chatter and noise died away. As I began to speak to them about the need for personal faith in God, they gradually became more serious; now the meeting was open for questions.

The club leader began. "I have a question to ask, but before I do let me make something quite clear. I am not a Christian; at least, I wouldn't call myself one. *But I am a genuine seeker.*"

I have forgotten now what his question was, but what I do remember is the picture of a thoughtful young man, honest enough to sum up his attitude to religion in general (and to Christianity in particular) by saying "I am a genuine seeker."

I believe that you are a seeker, too!

After all, you would probably not have read even this far unless you wanted to know the answers to the biggest questions of all—questions about God, life, religion, faith.

7

Perhaps you have never been a religious person, but the state of the world today, or something that has happened in your family or in your own life has made you begin to think about God.

Perhaps you were brought up to go to church or Sunday school but the day came when you stopped attending either. Now you are wondering whether there might be some value in them after all.

Perhaps you still go to church, but it seems deadly dull, without any real power or meaning—a performance, but not an experience.

Perhaps Christianity means nothing to you. Whenever you think of the church, you think only of a building where people are christened, married, or buried.

Perhaps you know somebody who is not just religious but claims to be a real Christian, and his life seems so obviously different from yours that it has begun to make you think.

Perhaps you *want* to believe, but you never seem to have time to think properly about religion, or to work it out in detail.

But you *are* a seeker!

This book is written for seekers—for people who want to give sensible and honest thought to the whole question of their relationship to God. It is not an examination of all the world's religions that ends by saying, "Now choose the one you like best." It is not a scientific textbook that turns religion into equations,

8

and faith into a formula. It is not a vague collection of various points of view.

It is a plain, straightforward book showing how a person who is honestly seeking for God can find Him.

This book is written for you!

1: The Truth

From now on I am going to quote frequently from the Bible and rely upon it for the basic truths of everything I say in this book. You may not believe in the Bible or may have doubts about much of it. That does not surprise me; many have the same difficulty, but genuine seekers will be prepared to look at what the Bible says. After all, if you want to locate a particular town, you look at a map of the region concerned; if you want to know a person's telephone number, you look in a telephone directory. Then surely if you want to know something about God and your relationship to Him, the sensible and honest thing to do is to look in the only book in the world that claims thousands of times to have God as its author.

That book is the Bible.

Perhaps you had not realized that the Bible spoke so plainly—but it does. Nearly 4,000 times in the Old Testament you will find words like "the Lord spoke," "the word of the Lord," "the Lord commanded," "the Lord said," "God spoke all these words," and so on.

When you turn to the New Testament you will find many similar statements there summed up like this:

> All scripture is given by inspiration of God, and is profitable for doctrine, for reproof, for correction, for instruction in righteousness (2 Timothy 3:16).*

But need we accept that? Could not the Bible have been written by very good men who wanted to spread their teaching throughout the world, or by wicked men writing with some evil motive? There has been no lack of ideas on the subject: somebody once calculated that between 1850 and 1910 critics of the Bible had advanced 747 explanations of its origin. Hardly any two agreed, and most were contradictory! Yet all the arguments against the divine authorship of the Bible fail to answer one simple piece of logic. John Wesley, who founded the Methodist Church in the 18th Century, put it like this:

> The Bible must be the invention either of good men or angels, bad men or devils, or of God. It could not be the invention of good men or angels, for they neither would nor could make a book and tell lies all the time they were writing it, saying "Thus saith the Lord" when it was their own invention. It could not be the invention of bad men or devils, for they could not

*Most of my quotations are from the King James Version of the Bible. For the sake of greater clarity I have sometimes employed two modern paraphrases, *The Amplified Bible* and *The Living Bible.* Other quotations are from the *New American Standard Bible,* © 1960, 1962, 1963, 1968, 1971, 1972, 1973, and 1975 by The Lockman Foundation, and are used by permission.

make a book that commands all duty, forbids all sin, and condemns their souls to hell for all eternity. Therefore the Bible must be given by Divine inspiration.

There are many other ways to show that the Bible is God's Word, but to list them all would take volumes. I ask you, as a genuine seeker, to accept the Bible's own claim that it is the Word of God, and to test that claim by following through its teachings with an open mind.

There are two important implications to the Bible's claim to be God's Word.

The Bible Is Completely True

Many people have the wrong idea about the Bible because they fail to understand what it is. It is a collection of 66 books, written by about 40 authors over a period of more than 1,600 years. It has one central theme, expressed in many different ways. It includes history, prophecy, poetry, biography, ethics, philosophy, and science; and in each of these the Bible is infallibly true. Take two examples.

The Bible contains a great deal of history. Is it accurate? Sir Isaac Newton, the father of modern science, had no doubts about it. He once said "There are more sure marks of authenticity in the Bible than in any profane history!" Again, listen to Professor Robert Dick Wilson of Princeton University, who spent 15 years studying Oriental languages and dialects, 15

years studying ancient inscriptions, and 15 years
studying ancient manuscripts and versions of the Bible. He says "The history given in the Bible is reliable,
but in profane documents there is an almost universal
inaccuracy and unreliability."

The Bible is not primarily a scientific textbook, although it does include statements that can be looked
at from a scientific point of view. Is its science accurate? Listen to Dr. Irwin Moon, Director of the Moody
Institute of Science, Los Angeles: "I have covered
every word from beginning to end many times, and,
so far as I know, there is not within the pages of this
book [the Bible] one single scientific inaccuracy, con-
tradiction, absurdity, or blunder."

No expert has ever disproved a single statement in
the Bible. What the Bible says on any subject is true!
And the Bible is primarily a book about God and our
relationship with Him—the subject that concerns you
at this very moment. This is how it is put in Psalm
19:7-9:

> The law of the Lord is perfect, converting the soul: the
> testimony of the Lord is sure, making wise the simple.
> The statutes of the Lord are right, rejoicing the heart:
> the commandment of the Lord is pure, enlightening
> the eyes. The fear of the Lord is clean, enduring for
> ever: the judgments of the Lord are true and righteous
> altogether.

The Bible Is Constantly True

Many people vaguely believe that the Bible is God's book, but suspect that it is now out of date. "After all," they say, "we live in a scientific age, and even the most recent parts of the Bible were written nearly 2,000 years ago." But why should that make it out of date? Truth can never change. One of my very young sons came home from school one day and said, "Daddy, do you know, two and two make three!" That was certainly new to me! I had to correct him and tell him that two and two made four, just as it did when I went to school, when my father went, and when my grandfather went, and just as it did before schools were ever founded. Truth never changes, and the Bible claims not only to be completely, but constantly true. "Concerning thy testimonies, I have known of old that thou hast founded them for ever" (Psalm 119:152). "The grass withereth, the flower fadeth: but the word of our God shall stand for ever" (Isaiah 40:8).

That answers the strange argument that science has disproved the Bible. How can truth disprove truth? None of the truth being discovered today through scientific research can disprove truth previously discovered, either in its own field or in any other. Men's theories and opinions constantly change, often in the light of new discoveries, but truth is united and final. If the Bible were a collection of men's ideas about religion—even the ideas of good and holy men—we might say that their ideas were now out of date or mistaken. But the human authors of these 66 books wrote by direct and divine inspiration in such a unique way that we can call the whole collection of books the Word of God, and God never changes.

Do you see the importance of that in your search for God? It means that God reveals Himself today through the pages of the Bible in such a way that He can be found and known. "So then faith cometh by hearing, and hearing by the word of God" (Romans 10:17). "The holy scriptures . . . are able to make thee wise unto salvation" (2 Timothy 3:15).

Are you a genuine seeker? Then put aside your prejudices and pre-conceived ideas, come to the Bible, and ask God to make its truth clear to you. Perhaps this prayer will help you to express your thoughts:

> *Almighty and eternal God, I am out of touch with You, and need to find You before my life can have real meaning. There are many things in the Bible that I do not understand. Enable me to come to it now with an open mind. Speak to me through what I read, showing me who You are, and how I can come to know You. Help me now to seek You with all my heart, and to find You.*

Is that what you want? Then stop and think it over carefully.

Now read that prayer again, making it your own, from the depths of your heart. But before you do, listen to this wonderful promise God makes to all who are in earnest in their search for Him: "And ye shall seek me, and find me, when ye shall search for me with all your heart" (Jeremiah 29:13).

2: The Problem

What does the word *religion* suggest to you? A church building perhaps? or stained-glass windows? or a priest dressed in a cassock and surplice? or somebody saying his prayers, or trying to lead a good life? a strange ritual or ceremony in a church, temple, or shrine?

Religion is universal, and everyone has some thoughts about it. The *Encyclopaedia of Religion and Ethics* has 13 enormous volumes, yet covers only a fraction of man's religious expressions. As William Blake once said, "Man must and will have some religion."

But why? What lies behind someone's remark that man is a religious animal?

The clue is in the word *religion*. It comes from two Latin words, *re* and *ligare*, meaning "to bind back." Religion is concerned with man's greatest need, which is to be "bound back" to God. Science, education, material possessions, or physical pleasure can never bring ultimate satisfaction to any man. Only when a man is "bound back" to God can he ever know complete fulfillment. As Augustine said long ago, "Thou madest us for Thyself and our hearts are restless until they rest in Thee."

Listen to the way in which biblical writers expressed that longing:

> My soul thirsteth for God, for the living God (Psalm 42:2).
>
> My heart and my flesh crieth out for the living God (Psalm 84:2).
>
> Shew us the Father [God], and it sufficeth us (John 14:8).

The recognition that a knowledge of God is man's greatest need leads us to think carefully about the problem of meeting it. As William James once wrote, "We and God have business with each other." But if finding God is the most important thing in life, why do so many people fail and go through life without a dynamic relationship with God?

What is the problem?

We saw earlier that *religion* means "binding back" and that man's greatest need is to be brought into touch with God. But is man really out of touch? Are we not all the children of God? Is the problem that serious? The right answers to these questions come as we look into the Bible and see something of the person, nature, and character of God and man.

What Is God?

In a recent book a modern writer shows that many people have a completely inadequate picture of God. They see Him as no more than a Resident Policeman, a parental hangover, or a Grand Old Man. For the truth, we turn to the Bible, and of the many things we learn about Him there, the following are among the most important statements to consider at the moment.

God is personal. God is not a "thing," an "it," a "power," or an "influence." He is the living God, who thinks, works, and feels. In the opening nine verses of Jeremiah 10 we read of the folly of men worshiping idols of wood and metal. Then we read, "But the Lord is the true God, he is the living God, and an everlasting king" (Jeremiah 10:10).

God is plural. Although there is only one God, He has revealed Himself to us in three distinct Persons, known together as the Trinity—the Father, the Son, and the Holy Spirit. That is impossible for any man to explain or understand, but the Bible states that each of the three Persons is truly and equally God. The Father is God—Ephesians 4:6 says that there is "One God and Father of all"; the Son is God—John 1:1 says that "the Word [Jesus]was God"; the Holy Spirit is God—He is described as "the Lord [who is] the Spirit" (2 Corinthians 3:18, NASB). Sometimes they are mentioned together, showing both equality and divinity, as in 2 Corinthians 13:14, which says, "The grace of the Lord Jesus Christ, and the love of God, and the communion of the Holy Ghost, be with you all. Amen."

God is eternal. To put It as simply as possible, He never had a beginning. He was neither created nor born, nor did He evolve. The Bible's first words are "In the beginning God . . . " (Genesis 1:1), and this same truth is emphasized in many other places, like these:

> Before the mountains were brought forth, or ever thou hadst formed the earth and the world, even from everlasting to everlasting, thou art God (Psalm 90:2).
>
> Thy kingdom is an everlasting kingdom, and thy dominion endureth throughout all generations (Psalm 145:13).
>
> I am Alpha and Omega, the beginning and the ending, saith the Lord, which is, and which was, and which is to come, the Almighty (Revelation 1:8).

God is independent. God is the only truly independent Being. His life was not given to Him. His power was not acquired. His wisdom was not learned. His knowledge was not gained. The apostle Paul once spoke of God's independence like this:

> God that made the world and all things therein, seeing that he is Lord of heaven and earth, dwelleth not in temples made with hands; neither is worshipped with men's hands, as though he needed any thing, seeing

that he giveth to all life, and breath, and all things
(Acts 17:24-25).

O the depth of the riches both of the wisdom and
knowledge of God! how unsearchable are his judgments, and his ways past finding out! For who hath
known the mind of the Lord? or who hath been his
counsellor? Or who hath first given to him, and it shall
be recompensed unto him again? For of him, and
through him, and to him, are all things: to whom be
glory for ever (Romans 11:33-36).

Here God is spoken of as the great, glorious, and
independent source of all life, wisdom, power, and
knowledge.

God is sovereign. King David of Israel has been
described as one of the greatest men who ever lived,
and it was he who said this:

Blessed be thou, Lord God of Israel our father, for ever
and ever. Thine, O Lord, is the greatness, and the
power, and the glory, and the victory, and the majesty:
for all that is in the heaven and in the earth is thine;
thine is the kingdom, O Lord, and thou art exalted as
head above all. Both riches and honour come of thee,
and thou reignest over all; and in thine hand is power
and might; and in thine hand it is to make great, and
to give strength unto all. Now therefore, our God, we
thank thee, and praise thy glorious name (1 Chroni-
cles 29:10-13).

We are taught here that God is sovereign over the
whole universe. He controls all the elements of time

and space. Paul says that God "worketh all things after the counsel of his own will" (Ephesians 1:11)—that is, God does whatever He wills, and nothing can prevent Him from so doing. With God there are no accidents or surprises. History is the outworking of God's unalterable will. The Bible teaches that God is in control, even of the evil that confronts us daily: "Our God is in the heavens: he hath done whatsoever he hath pleased" (Psalm 115:3). He is sovereign!

God is holy. He is completely without fault or defect, blemish, or stain. The word *holy* is the only description of God that is given triple force in the Bible. The prophet Isaiah once had a remarkable vision of God's glory, and he describes how he saw angels worshiping God and crying "Holy, holy, holy, is the Lord of hosts: the whole earth is full of his glory" (Isaiah 6:3). Other verses underline the same truth:

> Who is like unto thee, O Lord, among the gods? who is like thee, glorious in holiness, fearful in praises, doing wonders (Exodus 15:11).
> Exalt the Lord our God, and worship at his holy hill; for the Lord our God is holy (Psalm 99:9).
> God is light, and in him is no darkness at all (1 John 1:5).
> Who shall not fear thee, O Lord, and glorify thy name? for thou only art holy (Revelation 15:4).

What a breathtaking conception of God!—and the Bible tells us so much that we cannot mention here. God is all-wise; He has perfect knowledge of all things, past, present, and future; He is not limited by or to time and space; He is unchanging; He is perfectly righteous in all His dealings.

This is the God with whom we have to do!

Today, many people use God's name either as a swear word or as a joke. Others talk about Him lightheartedly or casually or as if He were their equal. They question His judgments, criticize His actions, blame Him when things go wrong. Surely this is dangerous ignorance.

What Is Man?

If man has too low a conception of God, he certainly has too high an opinion of himself! Recently, university students from Denmark and Yugoslavia debated whether civilization owes more to religion than to science. One speaker, arguing against religion, said, "Man, with science as his tool, has become the creator, master, and very essence of the universe." A casual glance at the world around us with its wars, bloodshed, hatred, violence, suffering, and multitude of unsolved problems should be enough to suggest that that is hardly a wise comment! The biblical picture is vastly different. Four words will help us to get what it says into focus. They are *dignity, disobedience, death,* and *depravity.* The first of these takes us back to the beginning of man's history.

Dignity. The Bible's account of man's beginning

could not be simpler: "God created man in his own image, in the image of God created he him; male and female created he them" (Genesis 1:27).

That means that man is not a refined ape or an accidental concoction of atoms, but he was made by God in a specific act of special creation. The word *created* is used only three times in Genesis 1, and each time it refers to the creation of something entirely new. The first, in verse 1, refers to all existence generally; the second, in verse 21, refers to all animal existence; and the third, in verse 27, refers to all human existence. Man is as different from all other animal existence as animal existence is from vegetable, or vegetable from mineral. Other animals do not have reason, conscience, coordinated intelligence, or any of the higher gifts of man. Man is the climax and crown of God's creation, with special power and authority. "And God blessed them, and God said unto them, Be fruitful, and multiply, and replenish the earth, and subdue it: and have dominion over the fish of the sea, and over the fowl of the air, and over every living thing that moveth upon the earth" (Genesis 1:28).

Man's dominion over other living creatures is not something he has gradually acquired by the law of the jungle over millions of years. It was something freely given to him by God.

Yet the first man was not only clearly *removed* from the rest of creation, but was also closely *related* to his

Creator. As the Bible puts it, "God created man in his own image" (Genesis 1:27). That does not mean that man was made the same shape or size as God, for "God is a Spirit" (John 4:24) and has neither shape nor size. Neither does it mean that man was a miniature replica of God, for God is eternal, whereas man had a specific beginning in time. What it does mean is that man was made in the moral likeness of God. He was holy, as God is holy. Man was created perfect, and although having free will and the ability to do wrong, he chose to do right, to be holy, to walk with God.

Perhaps the clearest way to grasp this is to notice what the Bible says in Genesis 1:31: "And God saw every thing that he had made, and, behold, it was very good." Here was the verdict of a holy, perfect God on His creation, including man: It was "very good." God was satisfied with man! They were in touch and tune one with each other! Such was the dignity of man's original state.

However, by the time we get to Genesis 6 we read "And God saw that the wickedness of man was great in the earth, and that every imagination of the thoughts of his heart was only evil continually" (Genesis 6:5). What had happened?

Disobedience. G. K. Chesterton wrote, "Whatever else is or is not true, this one thing is certain—man is not what he was meant to be." Why? Of the various explanations over the ages, only the Bible's clear statements fit the facts.

The Bible teaches that God not only created man in living fellowship with his Creator; He also gave him great freedom of action. "And the Lord God commanded the man, saying, Of every tree of the garden thou mayest freely eat" (Genesis 2:16).

This garden was obviously a wonderful place of amazing beauty. Everything that man needed for health and happiness was there in abundance, and God gave him authority and permission to take freely everything necessary for his enrichment and enjoyment. Yet God also gave man a specific warning. His first negative commandment: "But of the tree of the knowledge of good and evil, thou shalt not eat of it: for in the day that thou eatest thereof thou shalt surely die" (Genesis 2:17).

Exactly what the tree was and why God gave that commandment are questions that do not affect the issue here. What really matters is that just as the previous verse had been clear and full *permission,* so here there was clear and firm *prohibition*—"thou shalt not."

Genesis 3 tells us what happened next. The woman (later called Eve) was tempted by the devil, who appeared in the form of a serpent. "And when the woman saw that the tree was good for food, and that it was pleasant to the eyes, and a tree to be desired to make one wise, she took of the fruit thereof, and did eat, and gave also unto her husband with her; and he did eat" (Genesis 3:6).

For the very first time man had disobeyed God. He had previously lived a life of total obedience to the all-wise will of his Maker, walking in perfect communion with Him. Now, he had disobeyed. Sin had entered into human history. With what result?

Death. Do you remember what God's commandment had said? "But of the tree of the knowledge of good and evil, thou shalt not eat of it: for in the day that thou eatest thereof thou shalt surely die" (Genesis 2:17).

Man ate: did he die? that day?

As Adam and Eve were still alive the following day, and indeed for many years afterward, the answer would seem to be no. However, that would make God a liar and the remainder of the Bible unnecessary. The right answer to the question "Did man die when he first sinned?" comes only when we realize that death does not mean the end of life but *separation from life.* As Frederick P. Wood wrote, "Death means separation, not termination."

When God created man, He "breathed into his nostrils the breath of life; and man became a living soul" (Genesis 2:7). Man's God-given life was both physical and spiritual, and his relationship with God was maintained by complete obedience. When man disobeyed, that relationship was broken. *Man died that day*—he became separated from God—at the moment of his original sin. The Bible speaks of this death in two ways: as spiritual death and as physical death.

Spiritual death is the separation of the soul from God. This is stated very simply in the Bible. "And they heard the voice of the Lord God walking in the garden in the cool of the day: and Adam and his wife hid themselves from the presence of the Lord God amongst the trees of the garden" (Genesis 3:8).

Such a thing had never happened before. Until then Adam and Eve had been open and happy in the presence of their Maker; now they were terrified and ashamed. The broken command meant broken communion. By his deliberate disobedience man had cut himself off from God. Man died spiritually the moment he sinned, and we read, "Therefore the Lord God sent him forth from the garden of Eden" (Genesis 3:23).

Physical death is the separation of the soul from the body. Until his first sin, Adam was immortal. His relationship with God involved his whole being, body and soul. Now, he became the victim of disease, decay, and deterioration. He had been a living soul and a living body, in touch and tune with God, innocent and immortal; now he was a dead soul and a dying body, and his story ends with three inevitable words that underline the result of his disobedience: "And he died" (Genesis 5:5).

We now bring the story up to date. As we saw earlier, death is not the end, and just as death is the result of disobedience, so there is something that is the result of death.

Depravity. You may feel that you can read the
record of Adam and Eve's disobedience and their
spiritual and physical deaths, then close your Bible
and say "That had nothing to do with me." But you
cannot in fact do that, because of two verses in
Genesis 5, that bring the sin and separation of Adam
right into today's world and into your life:

> And Adam lived an hundred and thirty years, and
> begat a son *in his own likeness, after his image* . . .
> and he begat sons and daughters (Genesis 5:3-4,
> emphasis added).

These verses tell us plainly that during the remainder of their lives Adam and Eve had several children. In
the same chapter there is a family tree of Adam's
descendants until the days of Noah. Later, the family
tree continues to the days of Abraham, Isaac, and
Jacob. Twelve generations later we come to the great
King David, who lived about the year 1000 B.C. From
there, we come to the generations who lived toward
the end of the Old Testament times, and eventually to
the birth of John the Baptist at the beginning of the
New Testament. Less than thirty generations after
that, *you were born!*

That means that you and Adam are linked. You are
his direct descendant. Your family tree stretches back
in an unbroken line to the first man who ever lived on
the earth. But that is not all. Notice very carefully the
words I have emphasized in those verses from

Genesis 5: "And Adam . . . begat a son *in his own likeness, after his image."*

Do you remember where we met that kind of language before? It was in Genesis 1:27, where we read that "God created man *in his own image."* We saw that man was made in the moral likeness of God, a human reflection of the divine nature and character. He was holy, as God was holy. That same phrase, "after his image," is now used of Adam's first son and, by implication, of all his other sons and daughters. Adam's children—the first of whom was born after Adam had fallen into sin—shared Adam's nature and character; their state was the same as his in the sight of God. Adam's corrupt nature was thus transmitted to every generation that followed. He was cut off from God, separated by his sin, so as a result, all his children and descendants from that day on began their lives in the same condition. The Bible repeatedly makes this clear:

> Behold, I was shapen in iniquity; and in sin did my mother conceive me (Psalm 51:5).
>
> Therefore as sin came into the world through one man and death as the result of sin, so death spread to all men, (no one being able to stop it or to escape its power) because all men sinned (Romans 5:12, *The Amplified Bible*).
>
> We were then by nature children of (God's) wrath and heirs of (His) indignation, like the rest of mankind (Ephesians 2:3, *The Amplified Bible*).

Here is the obvious reason for the unrest, disorder, and wrongdoing of today's world. It results from the fact that all men are heirs of Adam, born with sinful natures. Blaise Pascal, the 17th-Century mathematical genius and religious philosopher, once said, "We are born unrighteous, for each one tends to himself, and the bent towards self is the beginning of all disorder."

Theologians call this "total depravity." It does not mean that every man is as bad as he can be or that man cannot tell right from wrong or that he is incapable of doing things that are helpful and pleasing to others. The word "depravity" means crookedness or perverseness; "total depravity" means that the crookedness and perversity have affected every part of man's nature, including his mind, will, affections, conscience, disposition, and imagination. In the simplest language, man is no longer centered on God; his nature is totally crooked and perverse. The Bible puts it like this:

> The heart is deceitful above all things, and desperately wicked: who can know it? (Jeremiah 17:9).
>
> For out of the heart proceed evil thoughts, murders, adulteries, fornications, thefts, false witness, blasphemies: These are the things which defile a man . . . (Matthew 15:19-20).
>
> Alienated from the life of God through the ignorance that is in them, because of the blindness of their heart (Ephesians 4:18).

> Even their mind and conscience is defiled (Titus 1:15).

We began this chapter by discovering that man's greatest need is to get right with God, the Creator and Sovereign of the universe, who is holy and righteous, and cannot even look upon sin.

Having discovered something of the nature and character of man, do you see the depth of your problem?

You were born away from God: you inherited a corrupt, fallen nature, affecting every part of your being. You are dead spiritually and dying physically. Before a holy and righteous God you are responsible for every sin that you have ever committed, guilty of deliberate disobedience.

The Bible says "For all have sinned, and come short of the glory of God" (Romans 3:23).

You have.

What can be done?

3: The Failure

What can be done?

If you have grasped what you have read so far, that is a question you must surely be asking. Born a sinner, corrupt in your nature, failing to come up to God's standards, you are spiritually separated from your Creator.

In the Bible's own words, you are one of those "having no hope, and without God in the world" (Ephesians 2:12).

Is there nothing you can do?

One of the greatest men of God who ever lived was the apostle Paul. Before getting right with God he lived a remarkable and varied life. A Roman citizen, he was born of Jewish parents and brought up in what is now southern Turkey. Later he entered the University at Jerusalem where his tutor, Gamaliel, was one of the leading educators of his day. While still a young man, Paul (he was called Saul at that time) became a private investigator for the Jewish religion and traveled all over the country rooting out heretics, flinging them into prison and sometimes even arranging their executions. Yet one thing dominated Saul's life from his earliest days—a concern to get right with God. When he finally did so, God used him to become one of His greatest-ever messengers, and to write at least 13 of the 27 books in the New Testament. In one of them, the epistle to the Philippians, Paul looks back on his life, describes his search for a living faith, and tells of the things on which he once relied to make him right with God. Because Paul is not only writing honest biography, but is also guided by the Holy Spirit, we need to be sure that we grasp what he is saying.

Here is the passage in question:

> We . . . have no confidence in the flesh. Though I might also have confidence in the flesh. If any other man thinketh that he hath whereof he might trust in the flesh, I more: circumcised the eighth day, of the stock of Israel, of the tribe of Benjamin, an Hebrew of the Hebrews; as touching the law, a Pharisee; concerning zeal, persecuting the church; touching the righteousness which is in the law, blameless. But what things were gain to me, those I counted loss (Philippians 3:3-7).

That may sound rather strange and remote from you and your need, but it is such an important passage that I want you to read it again, this time in a modern paraphrase called *The Living Bible,* by Kenneth N. Taylor, so that the more up-to-date style might help you to understand exactly what the passage means:

> We are helpless to save ourselves. Yet if anyone ever had a reason to hope that he could save himself, it would be I. If others could be saved by what they are, certainly I could! For I went through the Jewish initiation ceremony when I was eight days old, having been born into a pure-blooded Jewish home that was a branch of the old original Benjamin family. So I was a real Jew if there ever was one! What's more, I was a member of the Pharisees who demand the strictest obedience to every Jewish law and custom. And sincere? Yes, so much so that I greatly persecuted the church; and I tried to obey every Jewish rule and regulation right down to the very last point. But all these things that I once thought very worthwhile—now I've thrown them all away.

Is there anything you can *do* to make yourself right with God? Basically, all man's efforts through the years can be put into four groups—race, ritual, religion, and respectability. Drawing on his personal experience and with God-given insight into the truth, Paul mentions all four of them in this passage. Look carefully with me at each of them in turn and, as you look, remember that he is being directed to write by God the Holy Spirit. This is God's Word—*to you!*

Race. Paul says that he was "of the stock of Israel, of the tribe of Benjamin, an Hebrew of the Hebrews." What does that mean? Why is it important to you? The

Jewish nation was chosen by God to receive His Word and to share it with the rest of the world. As Paul says in Romans 3:2, "Unto them [the Jews] were committed the oracles of God." In that sense the Jews (or Hebrews) were God's chosen people, and almost inevitably as the years went on, they became very proud of their background. They began to look back to their great ancestors and to pride themselves on having such a wonderful heritage. They actually began to rely on their background to make them right with God.

Paul had done so. As he argued, he had not only been born into the pure stock of Israel, a descendant of Abraham (who was called "the Friend of God" [James 2:23]), but also of Isaac and Jacob. What is more, he traced his family tree back to the tribe of Benjamin, which had given Israel its first king. So he had a genuine claim to be "a real Jew if there ever was one!"

Yet he now realized that none of these advantages made him right with God. Of course they *were* advantages. As a child he would have been taught to believe in the one true God, he would have been taken regularly to a place of worship, he would have had the Scriptures read to him. Yet these did nothing to alter the fact that he was a descendant of Adam, born in Adam's fallen image, inheriting Adam's fallen nature, and therefore in the wrong with God from the very beginning of his life. In Paul's own words, "By one man [Adam] sin entered into the world, and death by sin; and so death passed upon all men, for that all have sinned" (Romans 5:12).

As somebody once put it, "Adam's blood courses in every man's veins. That blood carries with it a sentence of death. Adam rebelled against God; his bloodstream became poisoned, and every one of us as sons and daughters of Adam has blood poisoning. That's one way of describing the problem of the world today—blood poisoning."

Do you see how clearly this applies to you? However religious your background, however devout your parents, however godly your ancestors, the fact of the matter is that they, and you, were born in a state of sin, morally corrupt, away from God.

Your background, upbringing, and ancestry may have been a help to you in many ways, but they could never make you right with God. In that sense, race is a failure.

Ritual. Paul says that he was "circumcised the eighth day." Circumcision was an ancient Jewish ceremony, laid down by God's instructions in Genesis 17:9-14, and was to be carried out first upon Abraham and then upon all his male children, eight days after they were born, as a token of the special covenant made by God with Abraham at that time. Though it may all seem very strange to us today, to the ancient Jew it was an important sign of God's blessing upon Abraham and of His willingness to bless all those who followed in Abraham's spiritual footsteps. It was a sign, too, that Abraham was declared right with God, his sins forgiven and put out of the way. Yet for all that, the Bible makes it clear that the act of circumcision did not of itself make a person right with God. It was an outward and visible sign, but it did not automatically guarantee an inward and spiritual condition. Paul's own case proves the point. *He* had been circumcised when he was eight days old, and had for many years looked upon that as something that helped him to be right with God. Yet, later in life, when God opened his eyes to the truth, he saw quite plainly that it was possible to be a circumcised Jew without being a child of God at all, and that the only real evidence of a right relationship with God was a changed life. This is how he put it in his letter to the Christians at Rome:

Being a Jew is worth something if you obey God's laws; but if you don't, then you are no better off than the heathen. And if the heathen obey God's laws, won't God give them all the rights and honors he planned to give the Jews? In fact, those heathen will be much better off than you Jews who know so much about God and have his promises but don't obey his laws. For you are not real Jews just because you were born of Jewish parents or because you have gone through the Jewish initiation ceremony of circumcision. No, a real Jew is anyone whose heart is right with God. For God is not looking for those who cut their bodies in actual body circumcision, but he is looking for those with changed hearts and minds. Whoever has that kind of change in his life will get his praise

from God, even if not from you (Romans 2:25-29,
The Living Bible).

The lesson we learn from this passage is that no
man gets right with God by taking part in a ritual,
ceremony, or sacrament. Protestant churches have
generally practiced two sacraments: baptism and holy
communion. The Roman Catholic Church has seven:
baptism, confirmation, the mass, penance, extreme
unction, marriage, and orders, and teaches that most
of these are necessary or helpful for a person to obtain
salvation.

It is almost certain that at some time you have taken
part in one or another of these events. Perhaps you
were christened as a baby, or confirmed as an adoles-
cent. You may have taken holy communion or shared
in the mass, perhaps many times. You may have done
penance or offered some sacrifice for sin, or taken
part in some other religious ritual or ceremony in the
hope that it would make you right with God, or bring
you nearer to Him. That makes it vitally important that
at this very moment you should grasp this simple,
clear, biblical truth—that leaving on one side the
question whether any of these sacraments or ceremonies has biblical foundation or spiritual value, *not
a single one of them was ever divinely ordained to
make a man right with God,* and all of them together
have not succeeded in doing so for even one person in
all the world's history. In that sense, ritual is a failure!

Religion. The next thing that Paul tells us of his early search is that he was, "touching the law, a Pharisee; concerning zeal, persecuting the church."

We usually think of Pharisees in very critical terms, perhaps because the Bible speaks of some of them as hypocrites, and of others as being harsh, proud, envious or dishonest. Yet not all Pharisees were morally bad, and some had much to commend them. The Pharisees seem to have emerged in the 400 years between the Old and New Testaments. During that time many devout Jews fell away from their high standards of belief and behavior. A permissive society gradually developed, and it was against moral and religious looseness that the Pharisees took their stand. The name *Pharisee* means "separated one," speaking of their determination not to get dragged down with the trend of their times. They believed in one true and holy God, who ruled in all the affairs of men. They believed the Old Testament writings to be the Word of God and legally binding on all men who sought Him. They believed that relationship to God and obedience to God's laws were not only national issues, but personal matters for every individual. In New Testament times the Pharisees controlled the synagogues, and their whole lives could be said to be wrapped up in their religion. They strictly observed the forms and feasts laid down in the Old Testament. Some of them used to go without food two days a week, although the Old Testament law only required them to fast one day a year. They were very strict and regular in their giving to the church, and set aside at least one-tenth of their income to its work.

That background helps us to see exactly what Paul is saying here, because that is the tradition in which he was brought up. Giving evidence before the local court in Jerusalem, he said, "I am a Pharisee, the son of a Pharisee" (Acts 23:6). When being examined by King Agrippa, he claimed, "I have always been the strictest of Pharisees when it comes to obedience to Jewish laws and customs" (Acts 26:5, *The Living Bible*). Elsewhere, he went so far as to say "I was one of the most religious Jews of my own age in the whole country, and tried as hard as I possibly could to follow all the old, traditional rules of my religion" (Galatians 1:14, *The Living Bible*).

In a nutshell, Paul had been a deeply religious man all his life, and had practiced his religion with great sincerity and enthusiasm—so much so that when the Christians began what he considered to be a false sect, he persecuted them with every power at his disposal. Paul's religion, based (as he thought) on the Word of God, was something in which he believed with all his heart.

Now, he had come to see that it had failed him. It had not brought him into a real and living relationship with God.

A famous psychologist once said, "A man's religion is the audacious bid he makes to bind himself to creation and to his Creator. It is his ultimate attempt to enlarge and complete his personality by finding the supreme context in which he rightly belongs." In simpler words, religion is man's attempt to make himself right with God. But what the Bible teaches, from cover to cover, is that that attempt is always doomed to failure. As Paul himself puts it, "A man is not justified by the works of the law" (Galatians 2:16); in other words, a man is not reckoned or counted righteous before God because of his own works.

With his vast scientific and technological know-how, man can break out of earth's gravity and reach the moon, yet he cannot in his own strength break out of the spiritual gravity of his sinful nature and get in touch and tune with God. He has no power over the thrust of temptation, the grip of sin, the approach of death, the certainty of judgment. Dr. William E. Hocking, one-time Harvard Professor of Philosophy, declared bluntly, "Man brings himself up to a certain place and then finds that he hasn't the resources to complete himself. He must be completed from without by something beyond himself."

Now think what this means for you. Gather up in your mind all the religious activity you have ever performed—every church service you have ever attended, every prayer you have ever said, every word of Scripture you have ever read, every moment of time you have ever given to the service of the church, every penny you have ever donated to religious causes. The

Bible says that in terms of making you right with God, all of these are one hopeless failure. They did not, will not, and cannot make you acceptable in the sight of God. Even if you were to continue all of them with great regularity and sincerity to the end of your life, you would discover that you were still in the spiritually dead condition in which you were born. Now, that may hurt, but the Bible is perfectly plain, "By the deeds of the law there shall no flesh be justified in [God's] sight" (Romans 3:20).

In saying that religious activities do not make you right with God, I am *not* saying that in themselves they are wrong! It is *right* to go to church, to read the Bible regularly, to pray and to give. They are clearly commanded in God's Word. The danger is that we rely upon them to save us, when salvation is a God-given experience, not a man-made performance!

You may be saying at this point, "But I have found great help in going to church"; or "I have really felt God's presence while I was praying"; or "God seemed so real to me at one time." But is that sufficient? Is it enough that God *seemed* to be real to you, or that you *thought* you were getting through to Him? The Bible says "There is a way which seemeth right unto a man, but the end thereof are the ways of death" (Proverbs 14:12). You dare not take the risk of relying on feelings instead of facts! The plain truth is that religious activity cannot save you. Candles and confessions; invoca-

tions and incense; wine and wafers; services and sacraments; sprinkling and sacrifices—none of them can
remove sin or reconcile you to God. In that sense,
religion is a failure!

Respectability. The final thing Paul says about
himself in these verses in Philippians is that he was,
"touching the righteousness which is in the law,
blameless."

What exactly is he claiming? As we saw, the
Pharisees believed the Old Testament writings to be
God's word to man. But they were very concerned that
people got around some commandments by inter-
preting them to please themselves. To try to prevent
this, they set out their own very strict interpretations
and taught that in order to please God, one had to
obey every regulation down to the very last detail.

This was what Paul had been brought up to believe.
What is more, he could look back on his early days
and say in all honesty that he had been, "touching the
righteousness which is in the law, blameless."

These laws and traditions covered all kinds of religious, social, and moral behavior. They reached into
every part of a man's life, showing his need to be just,
honest, clean, upright, and related to God. This
means that, surrounded as he was by widespread
hypocrisy, immorality, dishonesty, greed, violence,
and selfishness, Paul had succeeded in reaching a
standard of respectability and goodness far in excess

of most people. He stood head and shoulders above most of his fellow men. Yet this too had been a failure! Just as his race, ritual, and religion had not brought him into living touch with God, so those years of striving to live a good, clean, upright life, had proved utterly futile.

You may feel that you have done many things that are good; that you have been kind, honest, helpful, generous, and so on. But in the light of the Bible's teaching you must now recognize that in terms of making you right with God even these acts are absolutely and utterly worthless. Now *please* do not misunderstand me here. I am not saying that you might as well give up trying to live a good life. It is obviously better to be pure than impure, honest than dishonest, unselfish than selfish, and so on—it *is* better, but not good enough to make you right with God!

Why not?

The Bible gives four answers to that question:

1. *Because God's law does not only concern our outward actions.* Paul deals with this in Romans 7, where he speaks of a man's responsibility to God's law. He says in verse 12 that "the law is holy, and the commandment holy, and just, and good," and in verse 14 he goes even further and declares, "For we know that the law is spiritual: but I am carnal, sold under sin."

What Paul is saying here is that the law makes demands not only on the outward behavior but also

on the inward and spiritual condition. It relates not
only to a man's words and actions, but also to his
thoughts, desires, motives, and aims. At a moment
when he had come face to face with reality in this
matter, David cried out to God, "Behold, You desire
truth in the inner being; make me therefore to know
wisdom in my inmost heart" (Psalm 51:6, *The
Amplified Bible*). That cry was a recognition of the
same truth, that God's law was inward and spiritual,
that it touched the very core of his being, and that
when it did so it found that core evil and corrupt.

Paul takes this truth to its logical conclusion in
Romans 8:8, where he says that "they that are in the
flesh cannot please God." Commenting on this,
Robert Haldane wrote, "An action may be materially
good in itself, but unless it proceed from a right
motive— the love of God—and be directed to a right
end—His glory—it cannot be acknowledged by
God."

God's law is spiritual. It probes beyond words and
actions, and when it does so we come face to face with
the plain fact stated in the Bible, "If we say that we have
no sin, we deceive ourselves, and the truth is not in us"
(1 John 1:8).

Even the best of our actions cannot meet the law's
inward demands.

2. *Because even our best is not good enough to
satisfy God.* Time and again people say to me "My
religion is, 'Do unto others what you would want them

to do to you.' " Others say, "To me, the great thing is
the Golden Rule" (which they say is the teaching given
in Matthew 5). Others say, "I try to follow the Bible's
teachings as best I can." All of them are really saying
the same thing: "I do my best." But are sincerity and
determined effort enough? Imagine yourself sitting
for an examination for which the pass mark is 70. For
months beforehand you study as hard as you can,
working far into the night. Then comes the examination. You read the questions and answer them to the
best of your ability. When the results are declared you
discover to your bitter disappointment that you scored
65 and failed. Of course, others failed. Some had less
than 50, others as little as 30. Not that that surprised
you, because they had been lazy and careless in their
study. But *you* had worked hard; *you* had done your
best. Now, if you would tell that to the examiner, would
he alter his verdict? Of course not! You had failed, *not*
because you did not get *any* marks or because you
had not done your best, but because your best did not
come up to the required standard.

Exactly the same is true in the matter of your relationship to God. You may have done your best—but it
is not good enough. God's law reflects His perfect
nature, and so perfection is the standard He lays
down. The question is not "Have I kept *most* of God's
laws?" but "Have I kept them *all*?" The man who aims
to get right with God by what the Bible calls "the works
of the law" would need to obey every single com-

mandment in the Bible from the beginning of his life to the end—and failure to do so condemns him. "For as many as are of the works of the Law are under a curse; for it is written, 'Cursed is every one who does not abide by all things written in the book of the Law, to perform them' " (Galatians 3:10, NASB).

It is vitally important that you should grasp this. If you are seeking and hoping to get right with God by your own efforts, you are striving for the impossible, because God's law demands perfect obedience in every part, something you have not rendered in the past and are not rendering now. To rely on our own efforts is to be condemned to failure.

3. *Because even one small sin is big enough to condemn us.* The Bible says, "For whosoever shall keep the whole law, and yet offend in one point, he is guilty of all" (James 2:10). The translation in *The Living Bible* makes it even plainer, "The person who keeps every law of God, but makes one little slip, is just as guilty as the person who has broken every law there is."

Obviously this does not mean that he is guilty of breaking every part of the law, *but that he is guilty of not keeping every part.*

An examination in school might list ten questions and then add "only six out of ten need be attempted." God's law does not operate like that, because it is one complete law, and the question you need to ask is not whether there are many parts of it you have kept, but

whether there are any you have broken. When one link
in a chain snaps, the whole chain is broken; one break
in a telegraph wire and communication is lost; one
puncture is sufficient to ruin a tire; one crack spoils a
pane of glass. Equally, one sin is sufficient to break
God's law. That makes the Bible's verdict clear and
unchallengeable, "If we say that we have no sin, we
deceive ourselves, and the truth is not in us" (1 John
1:8). We may not have sinned in the same way, or to
the same degree, or with the same knowledge of what
we were doing, but this much is certain: we have all
sinned, and one sin is enough to make us guilty in
God's sight and deserving of His judgment.

4. *Because even God's law is not strong enough to
save you.* We dare not overlook this fourth point.
God's law is summed up in the Ten Commandments, which form such a perfect basis for man's
religious and social life that the mayor of a large city,
speaking about the social and moral problems of our
times, said, "There are more than 2,000,000 laws on
the statute books. None of these would be needed if
the Ten Commandments were observed." But notice
that the Ten Commandments are laid down, not in
the first chapter of the Bible, but much later, in
Exodus 20:3-17. In other words, God's law is not
responsible for man's sin, but neither can it *remedy*
it! That was not the purpose for which it was given.
The Bible reveals a number of purposes for which
the law was given. It was given to reveal something of

God's nature and will, to promote the health and welfare of the human race, and to give reliable guidelines for God's people in their daily living. But supremely *the law was given to reveal the reality and nature of human sin.* Writing to the Christians at Rome, the apostle Paul said, "By the works of the Law no flesh will be justified in His sight; for through the Law comes the knowledge of sin" (Romans 3:20, NASB). Later, remembering his own discovery of the truth, he wrote, "I would not have come to know sin except through the Law; for I would not have known about coveting if the Law had not said, 'You shall not covet' " (Romans 7:7, NASB).

We find the same truth borne out today. Because man is born with an evil bias, his life is soon marked and marred by sin, and the law shows what sin really is—conflict with the nature, character, and will of a holy God. Just for a moment, place your life alongside the Ten Commandments or the Sermon on the Mount. What is the result, *honestly*? Is it not true that the straight-edge of the law shows you how crooked you are? The law demands honesty; you are dishonest. The law demands purity; you are impure. The law demands humility; you are proud. The law demands unselfishness; you are selfish. In short, the law demands that you love the Lord your God with all your heart, soul, mind, and strength, and that you love your neighbor as yourself. Can you honestly say that you do? The truthful answer to that question should make you see that in God's sight you are a guilty sinner—and the law will have pointed you to that truth. Here, then, is both the law's function and its limitation. It can diagnose but cannot deliver; it can reveal sin but cannot remedy it; it can show you how far away from God you are but cannot bring you any nearer to Him. To grasp this is to recognize how hopeless it is to trust in the law for salvation. Paul makes that perfectly clear, "For if a Law had been given which could confer (spiritual) life, then righteousness and right standing with God would certainly have come by Law" (Galatians 3:21, *The Amplified Bible*). In that sense, respectability is a failure!

We began this chapter as we ended the previous one, by seeing that man is born spiritually dead, morally corrupt, and cut off from God. Now we have seen that all of his efforts to remedy the situation end in the same way—failure.

Whatever your ancestry, background, or upbringing, whatever rituals and ceremonies you have performed, whatever religion you have followed, however sincerely you have tried to live a good life, the same facts remain. You are spiritually dead. You are morally corrupt. You are guilty before God. You are powerless to save yourself. And to all of that you must add this: every day brings you 24 hours nearer to the moment of death and to the day of judgment when God will finally banish every unsaved sinner from His pres-

ence forever and, in the Bible's own words, "The
wicked shall be turned into hell" (Psalm 9:17).

At this moment, that includes *you.*

Left as you are your case is hopeless.

You are lost.

4: The Answer

"God is love."

Somebody has said that those three words, which are found in 1 John 4:8 and 16, form "the most comprehensive and sublime of all biblical affirmations about God's being."

It is not just that God possesses love as one of His qualities, or that love is one of the things that God exercises, but rather that His very essence is love. God *is* love, and love governs His every activity.

Time and again in the Bible, God is recorded as giving certain people a personal assurance of His love toward them. For instance:

> "I have loved thee" (Isaiah 43:4).
>
> "I have loved thee with an everlasting love: therefore with lovingkindness have I drawn thee" (Jeremiah 31:3).
>
> "I have loved you, saith the Lord" (Malachi 1:2).

Yet the fullest evidence for the love of God comes from the wonderful record of that love *in action* right through the pages of the Bible.

Go back to the very beginning. Creation was an act of love. The last book in the Bible gives us this statement about the purpose behind creation: "Thou art worthy, O Lord, to receive glory and honour and power: for thou hast created all things, and for thy pleasure they are and were created" (Revelation 4:11). Because God is love, and creation was for His pleasure, we can know that it was an act of love. The same is true of the wonderful provision for all man's need in the Garden of Eden. All the atmospheric elements that made life both possible and pleasant; all the biological elements that supplied him with food to eat; these and every other provision came to man as the result of the love of God. Again, it was in love that God warned man of the one thing in the garden that would harm him, for He wanted him to know nothing less than the fullness of His blessing.

Then came man's disobedience. What then? Did God reject or destroy him? No! The Bible says that "God our Saviour . . . will have all men to be saved and to come unto the knowledge of the truth" (1 Timothy 2:3-4), and in harmony with His nature God acted to save man from the result of his own deliberate sin and rebellion. Writing centuries later, Paul said, "The grace of God that bringeth salvation hath appeared to all men" (Titus 2:11). The word *grace* means undeserved mercy. It is not just a kind thought, but love in action. It is something neither earned nor bought, but freely given. This fits in perfectly with all that we have seen so far. When man fell into sin he became guilty, lost, and helpless. Only God could bring man back into fellowship with Himself, and from that moment on the Bible is a record of the greatest rescue operation of all time—God saving guilty, lost, rebellious sinners who could not save themselves. That is the central message of the Bible.

Let me summarize it for you in the next few pages, but I should first give you a word of warning. You may feel that this is just ancient history with no direct importance for you. Nothing could be further from the truth. These pages could point *you* back to God and be the means of opening your understanding of God's way of salvation for the very first time. Read them carefully!

The Old Testament

After man's fall into sin, corruption spread throughout the human race; "God saw that the wickedness of man was great in the earth, and that every imagination of the thoughts of his heart was only evil continually" (Genesis 6:5). The Bible then records not only God's righteous judgment upon this sin, but also these vital words in Genesis 6:8, "Noah found grace in the eyes of the Lord." God having acted in perfect *justice* in punishing sin, now acted in great *love* in saving a man from the consequences of his sin, although he was as undeserving as the rest of humanity, and as incapable of saving himself as you and I.

Noah's story is simple but dramatic. God warned him of His just plan to flood the earth and instructed him to build an ark into which he was to take members of his family and a vast number of animals. It is then that for the first time we come across one of the most important words in the Bible. In promising to save those in the ark, God said to Noah, "With thee will I establish my covenant" (Genesis 6:18). A covenant is usually an agreement or bargain in which each party agrees to do something for the other, so that they will both benefit. But this covenant was different. It was a divine arrangement, not a human agreement. God declared that He would bless Noah and his family not because they suggested it or contributed to it, but simply because in His great love it pleased Him to do so.

God fulfilled His covenant, and while the rest of humanity perished, Noah and those in the ark were saved, giving us not only a remarkable chapter in human history, but also a vivid picture of God's dealings with men.

In Genesis 12 we meet the next outstanding man in Old Testament history, Abram (later called Abraham), and it is important to notice that God also established a covenant with him. However, that covenant went much further than the one made with Noah. First, the promises were much greater, including the granting to him and his successors of what became known as "the promised land" of Canaan, and reaching a wonderful climax in Genesis 17:8, where God says of Abraham and his successors, "I will be their God." Here, God promises to bring men back into a living relationship with Himself. Second, the covenant also went further in that it made special demands of personal faith and obedience upon Abraham and his successors. To gain the great spiritual blessings promised in the covenant, they had to believe what God had promised and do what God said. To fail would be to break the covenant.

The younger of Abraham's two sons was Isaac, and the Bible very carefully records God as promising "I will establish my covenant with him for an everlasting covenant" (Genesis 17:19).

Next, we trace the story to one of Isaac's sons, Jacob, whom God chose to inherit the great covenant blessings. One incident in Jacob's life is especially important. In Genesis 35:10 we read "And God said unto him, Thy name is Jacob: thy name shall not be called any more Jacob, but Israel shall be thy name: and he called his name Israel." This is important, because Jacob's large family gradually became known as "the children of Israel," and formed the original nucleus of the Jewish nation. Here is the clue to understanding the Jews as God's chosen people, inheriting the promises of the covenant made with Abraham, Isaac, and Jacob. They were chosen by God to carry His word to the rest of the world.

One of Jacob's sons, Joseph, was sold into Egypt

as a slave, but rose to favor there as a leading government official, and was later joined by his father and brothers. They prospered and grew in such a remarkable way that after the death of Joseph it is recorded that "the sons of Israel were fruitful and increased greatly, and multiplied, and became exceedingly mighty, so that the land was filled with them" (Exodus 1:7, NASB).

By now, there was a new ruler in Egypt, Rameses II, and he began to oppress the children of Israel, forcing them into slave labor. This went on for about 400 years. But God had not forgotten His people. By an unusual set of circumstances, a Hebrew boy called Moses was brought up in the Egyptian court at a time when the persecution against the Hebrews was so bitter that every new-born male child was ordered to be drowned. Some years later God called Moses to lead the Israelites from Egypt to the promised land of Canaan. The king (or Pharaoh) of Egypt repeatedly refused Moses' request to let the Israelites go, even after a series of nine national disasters, which God sent as judgments upon the Egyptians. Finally, in Exodus 12, God gave Moses instructions that were to have eternal significance.

The Israelites were told to prepare for a journey out of Egypt into the wilderness. The head of every household was to take an unblemished lamb, kill it, and sprinkle the blood on the lintel and doorposts of his house. That evening, the whole family was to eat the roast flesh of the lamb with unleavened bread and bitter herbs, and remain indoors until the morning. That night God promised to pass through the land in judgment and kill the firstborn child of every household not marked with the sprinkled blood: "The blood shall be to you for a token upon the houses where ye are: and when I see the blood, I will pass over you, and the plague shall not be upon you to destroy you, when I smite the land of Egypt" (Exodus 12:13). These two words—"pass over"—were to mean deliverance to the people of Israel, and they were commanded to commemorate the Passover annually from that day onward.

God acted exactly as He had promised. Death swept through the land. Every Egyptian household was affected, but every house sprinkled with the blood was safe. Immediately, the king summoned Moses and said, "Rise up, and get you forth from among my people, both ye and the children of Israel; and go, serve the Lord, as ye have said" (Exodus 12:31). The people of Israel were free, delivered by the hand of God in fulfillment of His covenant with their forefathers.

This vast company—about 600,000 men, besides women and children—now began to travel through the wilderness, and after three months they came to Mount Sinai. It was here that God, through Moses, reminded them of His covenant, and the people made a solemn vow to obey, "And all the people answered together, and said, All that the Lord hath spoken we will do" (Exodus 19:8).

God then gave the people the Ten Commandments, based on the fact that He was their sovereign Lord. These laid down the basic rule of life expected from His covenant people. Read them through now, and remind yourself of their solemnity and high demands:

> Then God spoke all these words, saying, "I am the LORD your God, who brought you out of the land of Egypt, out of the house of slavery.
>
> "You shall have no other gods before Me.
>
> "You shall not make for yourself an idol, or any likeness of what is in heaven above or on the earth beneath or in the water under the earth.
>
> "You shall not worship them or serve them; for I, the Lord your God, am a jealous God, visiting the iniquity of the fathers on the children, on the third and the fourth generations of those who hate Me, but showing lovingkindness to thousands, to those who love Me and keep My commandments.
>
> "You shall not take the name of the Lord your God in vain, for the Lord will not leave him unpunished who takes His name in vain.
>
> "Remember the sabbath day, to keep it holy.
>
> "Six days you shall labor and do all your work, but the seventh day is a sabbath of the Lord your God; in it you shall not do any work, you or your son or your daughter, your male or your female servant or your cattle or your sojourner who stays with you.

"For in six days the Lord made the heavens and the earth, the sea and all that is in them, and rested on the seventh day; therefore the Lord blessed the sabbath day and made it holy.

"Honor your father and your mother, that your days may be prolonged in the land which the Lord your God gives you.

"You shall not murder.

"You shall not commit adultery.

"You shall not steal.

"You shall not bear false witness against your neighbor.

"You shall not covet your neighbor's house; you shall not covet your neighbor's wife or his male servant or his female servant or his ox or his donkey or anything that belongs to your neighbor" (Exodus 20:1-17, NASB).

God gave many other instructions at Sinai, and we must take special notice here of two of them.

First, to provide a way of forgiveness man himself could never achieve, an animal was to be used as a substitute in bearing the sin of a man who truly sought forgiveness. By placing his hand on the head of the animal to be sacrificed, the sinner transferred his guilt from himself to the animal, and God's judgment upon sin was transferred to the innocent victim or substitute.

Second, for sin's death penalty to be paid without destroying the sinner, God ordained the sacrificial death of an animal as a substitute, and when this was done, God graciously accepted the offering in the place of the death of the sinner. We shall see the significance of this shortly, when we turn to the New Testament.

These sacrifices, and many other rituals and ceremonies given at this time, had to be repeated, either at regular intervals as laid down by God, or when the need for them arose.

The rest of the Old Testament story covers a period of about 800 years. It is fascinating history, but the one central thing we need to notice from it is that through all the ebb and flow of Israel's fortunes, *God continued to speak* through men of His choice. He continually reminded His people of both His law and His love. The most important of the messengers for us to bear in mind here were the *prophets*, men divinely inspired to proclaim God's word and sometimes to foretell events that were to happen in the future. Some were national events, some local, but one dominated them all. Through the prophets God promised to intervene in history in an entirely new and different way by sending to earth a Person who would bring the complete and final answer to man's greatest need, the need to be delivered from sin and made right with God.

We cannot list all the relevant prophecies here, but these six, the first going right back to God's direct word to man in the Garden of Eden, show how, as time went on, more and more detail was added about this coming deliverer.

He would be a human being, born of a woman. In Genesis 3:15, speaking to the tempter who had lured Adam and Eve into sin, God said, "I will put enmity between thee and the woman, and between thy seed and her seed; it shall bruise thy head, and thou shalt bruise his heel."

He would be a descendant of Abraham. In Genesis 12:3 God promised Abraham, "In thee shall all families of the earth be blessed."

He would come from the tribe of Judah. In Genesis 49:10 Jacob, on his deathbed, was inspired to make this prophecy about Judah, one of his twelve sons: "The sceptre shall not depart from Judah, nor a lawgiver from between his feet, until Shiloh come; and unto him shall the gathering of the people be."

He would come from the house of David. In 2 Samuel 7:13 the prophet Nathan told David that from his family a great king should come of whom God promised, "He shall build an house for my name, and I will stablish the throne of his kingdom for ever."

He would be born of a virgin. In Isaiah 7:13-14 God promised to King Ahaz, "Hear ye now, O house of David, . . . the Lord himself shall give you a sign; behold, a virgin shall conceive, and bear a son, and shall call his name Immanuel." *(Immanuel* means "God with us.")

He would be born in Bethlehem. In Micah 5:2 God promised: "But thou, Bethlehem Ephratah, though thou be little among the thousands of Judah, yet out of thee shall he come forth unto me that is to be ruler in Israel; whose goings forth have been from of old, from everlasting."

The way was gradually being prepared for the great moment.

From the end of the Old Testament there was silence for 400 years.

The New Testament

The New Testament opens in the same way that the Old Testament closes—with the voice of a prophet. This time his name is John, generally known as John the Baptist because of his practice of baptizing those who showed genuine evidence of wanting to turn to God. John's message was essentially the same as that of the Old Testament prophets—he called on men to change their ways, to repent: but he also added a new, urgent note, "The kingdom of heaven is at hand" (Matthew 3:2). The impact of his preaching was such that people began to ask him whether he was the promised deliverer. He replied, "I am not the Christ" (John 1:20). (The word *Christ* is the Greek equivalent of the Hebrew word *Messiah*, which means "anointed one," a name the Jews gave to the expected deliverer.) John claimed only to be the Messiah's forerunner promised by the prophet Isaiah, "I am the voice of one crying in the wilderness, Make straight the way of the Lord" (John 1:23). But at the same time he made it clear that the promised deliverer had already been born and was living among them, "There standeth one among you, whom ye know not; he it is, who coming after me is preferred before me, whose shoe's latchet I am not worthy to unloose" (John 1:26-27).

The next day Jesus, who lived in the town of Nazareth, joined those crowding to hear John's preaching. In a moment of great drama, John suddenly pointed to Jesus and said, "Behold the Lamb of God, which taketh away the sin of the world" (John 1:29). To the Jewish people, with their knowledge of Old Testament history, the covenant made with their fathers, the principle of an animal substitute as a sacrifice for sin, and the message of the prophets, this meant only one thing—a claim that Jesus was the Messiah, the Christ, the promised Savior of the world, God's complete answer to man's greatest need.

If you have read this book carefully so far, you will realize that at this point your search for God hinges on one crucial question: *was John's statement true or false?* If it was false, then you must look elsewhere for the answer to your need; if it was true, then Jesus *is* the answer! We must now look carefully at the evidence we find about Jesus in the New Testament.

HIS DESCENT

The matter of His descent is obviously vital, as the prophecies about the Messiah were clear and emphatic. Did Jesus fulfill them? Let us check the six we noted earlier—

A human being, born of a woman. Recording the birth of Jesus, the Bible says of His mother Mary, "The days were accomplished that she should be delivered. And she brought forth her first born son" (Luke 2:6-7). Jesus was born by normal human process.

A descendant of Abraham. Jesus' family tree in Matthew 1 traces His ancestors back to Abraham.

From the tribe of Judah. In the same family tree, only one of Jacob's sons is named—Judah (Matthew 1:2).

From the house of David. Again, the same family tree carefully and accurately includes "David the king" (Matthew 1:6).

Born of a virgin. While she was engaged to Joseph, the man later to become her husband, Mary had an extraordinary visit from an angel, who told her that she was to give birth to a son. The message went on: "And thou shalt call his name JESUS. He shall be great, and shall be called the Son of the Highest: and the Lord God shall give unto him the throne of his father David: and he shall reign over the house of Jacob for ever; and of his kingdom there shall be no end" (Luke 1:31-33). When Joseph discovered that Mary was pregnant, and knew that he was not responsible, he wanted to break off the engagement, but God spoke to him in a dream and said, "Joseph, son of David, do not be afraid to take Mary as your wife; for that which has been conceived in her is of the Holy Spirit. And

she will bear a Son; and you shall call His name Jesus,
for it is He who will save His people from their sins"
(Matthew 1:20-21, NASB). To emphasize the importance of this, Matthew adds, "All this took place that
what was spoken by the Lord through the prophet
might be fulfilled, saying, 'Behold, the virgin shall be
with child, and shall bear a Son, and they shall call His
name Immanuel,' which translated means, 'God with
us' " (Matthew 1:22-23, NASB).

Born in Bethlehem. At the time of Jesus' birth,
Mary and Joseph lived in the town of Nazareth, but the
occupying Roman authorities ordered a census that
required the head of each household to register in the
city of his ancestry. We then read: "And all went to be
taxed, every one into his own city. And Joseph also
went up from Galilee, out of the city of Nazareth, into
Judaea, unto the city of David, which is called
Bethlehem; (because he was of the house and lineage
of David:) to be taxed with Mary his espoused wife,
being great with child. And so it was, that, while they
were there, the days were accomplished that she
should be delivered. And she brought forth her
firstborn son" (Luke 2:3-7).

In His line of descent, and in the details of His
conception and birth, Jesus fulfilled all the prophecies
made about the promised Messiah.

HIS DEEDS

The Bible records little about the earthly life of

Jesus until John points Him out as the Messiah at the beginning of His public life. Over the next three years He was to make a greater impact than any other man in history.

One of His biographers went so far as to say, "And there are also many other things which Jesus did, the which, if they should be written every one, I suppose that even the world itself could not contain the books that should be written" (John 21:25).

Let us list some of them. He healed "all manner of sickness and all manner of disease among the people" (Matthew 4:23). Blindness, deafness, paralysis, illnesses connected with the blood, diseases of the nervous system, organic disorders of many kinds, all were healed. Almost all the healings were instantaneous, and there is no recorded case of a relapse. Some who came to Him were demon-possessed, and the demons were cast out with the same authority and power displayed in His other miracles. On at least three occasions He brought a dead person back to life: a twelve-year-old girl (Mark 5:21-43); a man in the village of Nain (Luke 7:11-17); and a personal friend called Lazarus, who had been buried four days before Jesus arrived (John 11:1-46).

Jesus revealed the same power over the natural elements. At a wedding feast, He miraculously changed water into wine (John 2:1-11). Once He fed a crowd of over 5,000 hungry people with a handful of bread and fish (Matthew 14:13-21); on another occasion He did the same for a crowd of over 4,000 (Matthew 15:32-39). He told experienced fishermen exactly where fish could be caught (Luke 5:1-11). One word from Him brought an immediate end to a storm so violent that hardened sailors were terrified of drowning (Mark 4:35-41).

Inevitably, He attracted enormous publicity, and soon a critical question arose. After He had healed a paralytic and told him that his sins were forgiven, the Pharisees asked "Who is this which speaketh blasphemies? Who can forgive sins, but God alone?" (Luke 5:21). Later, after He had claimed to forgive the sins of a notoriously immoral woman, the same question was asked, "Who is this that forgiveth sins also?" (Luke 7:49). When Herod Antipas, then ruling Galilee, heard reports of Jesus, he asked, "Who is this, of whom I hear such things?" (Luke 9:9). On His final visit to Jerusalem, we are told that "All the city was moved, saying, Who is this?" (Matthew 21:10).

That is the crucial question. Earlier, we noted a prophecy that referred to the coming Messiah as "Immanuel," meaning "God with us," indicating that God Himself would come to be the Savior of men. Isaiah said the same thing in this way: "For unto us a child is born, unto us a son is given: and the government shall be upon his shoulder, and his name shall be called Wonderful, Counsellor, The mighty God, The everlasting Father, The Prince of Peace. Of the increase of his government and peace there shall be no end, upon the throne of David, and upon his kingdom, to order it, and to establish it with judgment and with justice from henceforth even for ever. The zeal of the Lord of hosts will perform this" (Isaiah 9:6-7).

HIS DECLARATIONS

It is impossible to read the New Testament without noticing how much Jesus spoke about Himself. As John R. W. Stott has pointed out in his book *Basic Christianity*, "This immediately sets Him apart from all the other great religious teachers of the world. They are self-effacing; He is self-advancing. They point away from themselves and say 'That is the truth, so far as I perceive it; follow that.' Jesus says 'I am the truth, follow me.' The founder of none of the ethnic religions has dared to say such a thing."

Let us look at some of the declarations Jesus made about Himself.

His origin. Although born normally, He claimed that His life did not begin at Bethlehem. In John 6:38 He said "I came down from heaven." In John 8:23 He told the Jewish crowds, "Ye are from beneath; I am from above: ye are of this world; I am not of this world." In John 8:42 He added, "I proceeded forth and came from God." He deliberately set Himself apart from the rest of humanity.

His fulfillment of the Old Testament prophecies.

The New Testament writers repeatedly show Jesus as fulfilling Old Testament prophecies, and it is quite obvious that He agreed with this. On one occasion He said, "You search the Scriptures, because you think that in them you have eternal life; and it is these that bear witness of Me" (John 5:39, NASB). In other words, He claimed that the Old Testament pointed to Him. Again, during a service at the synagogue in Nazareth He read aloud from an Old Testament prophecy about the Messiah in Isaiah 61:1-2: "The Spirit of the Lord is upon me, because he hath anointed me to preach the gospel to the poor; he hath sent me to heal the brokenhearted, to preach deliverance to the captives, and recovering of sight to the blind, to set at liberty them that are bruised, to preach the acceptable year of the Lord" (Luke 4:18-19). With everybody's attention riveted on Him, He went on, "This day is this scripture fulfilled in your ears" (Luke 4:21). His meaning could not have been clearer.

His miracles. There had been isolated miracles in the Old Testament, but Jesus carried out what has been called "a wholesale onslaught on the forces of evil and disease." The other important difference was that whereas the Old Testament never pointed to the person performing them, Jesus made it clear that *His* miracles did so: "The works that I do in my Father's name, they bear witness of me" (John 10:25).

His teaching. Few would question that the moral teaching of Jesus is of the highest quality ever known.

Even His enemies admitted, "Never man spake like this man" (John 7:46). But it was not merely *what* He said but *how* He spoke that startled people. They were impressed not only with the *quality* of His words, but with their *authority*. At the end of His Sermon on the Mount, we read, "The multitudes were amazed at His teaching; for He was teaching them as one having authority, and not as their scribes" (Matthew 7:28-29, NASB). At Capernaum, "They were astonished at his doctrine: for his word was with power" (Luke 4:32). Yet Jesus Himself, speaking about events leading up to the end of the world, surpassed even those claims by saying, "Heaven and earth shall pass away, but my words shall not pass away" (Matthew 24:35). He claimed that His words were eternally true, relevant for all time and incapable of being contradicted!

His character. Truly spiritual men are reluctant to commend themselves. The more they recognize the holiness and majesty of God, the more they realize their own sin and weakness. The apostle Paul, for instance, writes "I am the least of the apostles, who am not fit to be called an apostle" (1 Corinthians 15:9, NASB). Yet Jesus, who was constantly teaching humility, repeatedly declared that He was sinless. Once, He put it like this, "I do always those things that please him [God]" (John 8:29). When He challenged religious and critical Jews, "Which one of you convicts me of sin?" (John 8:46, NASB), they replied that He was mad—but they had no answer to His question!

Again, referring to the power of the devil over ordinary men, He said, "He has nothing in Me" (John 14:30, NASB). In relation to the law of God, the lives of others, and the temptations of the devil, Jesus constantly claimed to be faultless.

Were those claims borne out by others?

Two of His closest friends, Peter and John, lived with Him for three years, and were well able to assess Him. What is their testimony? Peter says that Jesus was "without blemish and without spot" (1 Peter 1:19) and that He "did no sin, neither was guile found in his mouth" (1 Peter 2:22). John's words are just as concise and clear: "In him is no sin" (1 John 3:5). Paul says of Jesus that He was one "who knew no sin" (2 Corinthians 5:21). The writer of the epistle to the Hebrews says of Jesus that He "was in all points tempted like as we are, yet without sin" (Hebrews 4:15). The same writer also declares Jesus to have been "holy, innocent, undefiled, separated from sinners" (7:26, NASB) and that He was "without spot" (9:14).

Then there are the statements of His enemies during the hours surrounding His arrest, trial, and execution. Pontius Pilate, the Roman judge, said "I find no fault in this man" (Luke 23:4), and later, "I, having examined him before you, have found no fault in this man touching those things whereof ye accuse him" (Luke 23:14), and finally, "What evil hath he done? I have found no cause of death in him" (Luke 23:22).

Pilate's wife, as the result of a strange dream, sent her husband a message, "Have thou nothing to do with that just man" (Matthew 27:19). A thief being executed at the same time said, "This man hath done nothing amiss" (Luke 23:41). Judas Iscariot, who betrayed Jesus to the authorities, suddenly realized his crime and cried, "I have sinned in that I have betrayed the innocent blood" (Matthew 27:4), while one of the Roman soldiers responsible for carrying out the execution gave the final verdict, "Certainly this was a righteous man" (Luke 23:47).

All these witnesses underlined Jesus' own declaration that His character was perfect.

His uniqueness. In the plainest way, Jesus claimed that there had never been His equal in the history of the world, nor would such a person ever appear again. He was unique, and every other person in history would need to assess his life in the context of His person, life, work, and teaching. Here are some of these claims in what have been called "The *I Am's* of John's Gospel":

> I am the bread of life: he that cometh to me shall never hunger; and he that believeth on me shall never thirst (John 6:35).
>
> I am the light of the world: he that followeth me shall not walk in darkness, but shall have the light of life (John 8:12).

I am the door: by me if any man enter in, he shall be
saved, and shall go in and out, and find pasture"
(John 10:9).

I am the resurrection, and the life: he that believeth in
me, though he were dead, yet shall he live: and
whosoever liveth and believeth in me shall never die
(John 11:25-26).

I am the way, the truth, and the life: no man cometh
unto the Father but by me (John 14:6).

I am the true vine, and my Father is the hus-
bandman (John 15:1).

No mere man could make these claims unless he
was insane or blasphemous. They make sense only if
the speaker was God in human form. Did Jesus actually claim *that?* Let us look at a last group of His
declarations.

His nature. There is no doubt about what Jesus
believed and taught about His nature.

First, He used God's name as His own. On one
occasion, Jewish leaders, angry at the extravagant
claims Jesus made, asked Him, "Art thou greater than
our father Abraham?" (John 8:53) and went on,
"Thou art not yet fifty years old, and hast thou seen
Abraham?" (John 8:57). Jesus replied, "Verily, verily, I
say unto you, Before Abraham was, I am" (John 8:58).
The last two words are most important. If Jesus was
only claiming to have been older than Abraham—and
that would have been amazing enough!—He would

have said "Before Abraham was, *I was*." Instead, He
deliberately used the words *"I am*." To discover why,
we must go back to the Old Testament. When called
by God to lead the Israelites out of Egypt, Moses asked
by what name he should identify God to the children
of Israel. God's answer is recorded in Exodus 3:14,
"And God said unto Moses, I AM THAT I AM: and he
said, Thus shalt thou say unto the children of Israel, I
AM hath sent me unto you." To the devout Jew, this
remained one of God's distinctive names, and to hear
Jesus (who was also a Jew and knew its meaning
perfectly well) using it as His own was too much. It was
blasphemy and demanded death by stoning, "Then
took they up stones to cast at him" (John 8:59). It is
obvious from this that both Jesus and the Jews knew
the implication—Jesus claimed the right to use God's
name as His own, as He did again in John 13:13 and
John 18:5.

Second, He claimed to be equal with God. He did
this so often and so naturally that we need only list His
words as clear evidence:

> Whosoever shall receive me, receiveth not me, but
> him that sent me (Mark 9:37).
> He that honoureth not the Son honoureth not the
> Father which hath sent him (John 5:23).
> If ye had known me, ye should have known my
> Father also (John 8:19).
> I and my Father are one (John 10:30).

He that believeth on me, believeth not on me, but on him that sent me (John 12:44).

He that seeth me seeth him that sent me (John 12:45).

If ye had known me, ye should have known my Father also (John 14:7).

He that hath seen me hath seen the Father (John 14:9).

Believe me that I am in the Father, and the Father in me (John 14:11).

He that hateth me hateth my Father also (John 15:23).

Nothing could be plainer. Jesus claimed to be God, and His whole life proved the truth of His claim.

Again, this is borne out by the witness of others. John, describing Jesus as "the Word," says, "In the beginning was the Word, and the Word was with God, and the Word was God" (John 1:1), adding, "And the Word was made flesh, and dwelt among us" (John 1:14). Paul speaks of Christ as being "over all, God blessed for ever" (Romans 9:5) and as being "the image of the invisible God" (Colossians 1:15); he says that "in him dwelleth all the fulness of the Godhead bodily" (Colossians 2:9) and that "God was manifest in the flesh" (1 Timothy 3:16); he describes Him as "Our Lord Jesus Christ . . . the blessed and only Potentate, the King of kings and Lord of lords" (1 Timothy 6:14-15).

All this evidence points to only one conclusion,

"This is indeed the Christ, the Saviour of the world" (John 4:42).

We saw earlier that the Old Testament covenant and sacrifices were only temporary and looked forward to a *new covenant.* God had promised, "Behold, the days come, saith the Lord, that I will make a new covenant with the house of Israel, and with the house of Judah" (Jeremiah 31:31) and He said that it would be a covenant so effective that, as far as those included in it were concerned, "I will forgive their iniquity, and I will remember their sin no more" (Jeremiah 31:34).

Bearing that in mind, we come to the tremendous statement in Hebrews 12:24, which says that Jesus is the "mediator of the new covenant." The function of a mediator is to bring together two separated parties, and the Bible teaches that that is why Jesus came, to bring men back into fellowship with God through this new covenant. That is why the second part of the Bible is called "The New Testament of our Lord and Saviour Jesus Christ"—the word *testament* means "covenant." Jesus said, "The Son of man is come to seek and to save that which was lost" (Luke 19:10); "For God sent not his Son into the world to condemn the world; but that the world through him might be saved" (John 3:17); "I came not to judge the world, but to save the world" (John 12:47). Paul confirmed it, "This is a faithful saying, and worthy of all acceptation, that Christ Jesus came into the world to save sinners" (1

Timothy 1:15); and John added, "Ye know that he was manifested to take away our sins" (1 John 3:5). How was this accomplished?

We can summarize the New Testament by saying that the four gospels are the biographies of Jesus, the book of Acts tells us about the years immediately after His death, the epistles give us the teaching that follows from all this, and the final book in the Bible, Revelation, sometimes in symbolic language, includes events relating to the end of the world.

The remarkable thing about the New Testament is that it concentrates so much on the death of Jesus. It has been said that about two-fifths of the gospel of Matthew, three-fifths of the gospel of Mark, one-third of the gospel of Luke, and nearly one-half of the gospel of John record the events surrounding the week Jesus was crucified. The apostles had the same emphasis. Paul, for instance, said, "God forbid that I should glory, save in the cross of our Lord Jesus Christ" (Galatians 6:14); "I determined not to know anything among you, save Jesus Christ, and him crucified" (1 Corinthians 2:2); and "I delivered to you as of first importance what I also received, that Christ died for our sins according to the Scriptures" (1 Corinthians 15:3, NASB). The New Testament consistently emphasizes the death of Jesus as being "of first importance," and the final word comes from Jesus, who, speaking about His death, said "For this cause came I unto this hour" (John 12:27). Jesus said that

His birth, life, teaching, and miracles were all pre-
paratory to the one great purpose of His coming to
earth—His death. What was so important about it?

HIS DEATH

First, the death of Jesus was voluntary. Clearly
He *ought* not to have died, as He was innocent
of the false charges brought against Him. Further-
more, He *need* not have died. He had power to over
come all those who sought to destroy Him. In John
10:18 He said of His own life, "No man taketh it from
me, but I lay it down of myself. I have power to lay it
down, and I have power to take it again." At His arrest,
Peter drew a sword and attacked one of those making
the arrest, but Jesus stopped him, adding, "Thinkest
thou that I cannot now pray to my Father, and he shall
presently give me more than twelve legions of
angels?" (Matthew 26:53). The point is plain—Jesus
volunteered to die. Yet, in one sense, He *had* to die, for
it was the heart of God's plan of salvation. The Old
Testament prophecies included many about His
death. Here are some, listed alongside the New Testament record of what actually happened.

"They gave me also gall for my meat; and in my thirst they gave me vinegar to drink" (Psalm 69:21).

"They gave him vinegar to drink mingled with gall" (Matthew 27:34).

"He was numbered with the transgressors" (Isaiah 53:12).

"Then were there two thieves crucified with him, one on the right hand, and another on the left" (Matthew 27:38).

"I became also a reproach unto them: when they looked upon me they shaked their heads" (Psalm 109:25).

"And they that passed by reviled him, wagging their heads" (Matthew 27:39).

"He . . . made intercession for the transgressors" (Isaiah 53:12).

"Then said Jesus, Father, forgive them; for they know not what they do" (Luke 23:34).

"They pierced my hands and my feet" (Psalm 22:16).

"And they crucified him" (Matthew 27:35).

"They part my garments among them, and cast lots upon my vesture" (Psalm 22:18).

"And when they had crucified him, they parted his garments, casting lots upon them, what every man should take" (Mark 15:24).

"He keepeth all his bones: not one of them is broken" (Psalm 34:20).

"Then came the soldiers, and brake the legs of the first, and of the other which was crucified with him. But when they came to Jesus, and saw that he was dead already, they brake not his legs" (John 19:32-33).

In this amazing fulfillment of prophecies written hundreds of years beforehand, God's plan was carried out according to His perfect will. As Peter said, "This Man, delivered up by the predetermined plan and foreknowledge of God, you nailed to a cross by the hands of godless men and put Him to death" (Acts 2:23, NASB).

How could the death of Jesus be inevitable yet voluntary? There is only one explanation—God's will was His will. Although as a man He shrank from the terrible agony, He nevertheless "became obedient unto death, even the death of the cross" (Philippians 2:8), according to His own divine, eternal will.

Second, the death of Jesus was vicarious. It was in the place of others. There is a second reason He need not have died: as He was without sin, death had no claim on Him. Death is the result of sin, but as Jesus had no sin of His own, He must have died for the sins of others, taking their place, bearing the penalty and punishment for their sin. This is confirmed in the Old Testament, the words of Jesus, and the teaching of the apostles:

The Old Testament

"The reproaches of them that reproached thee are fallen upon me" (Psalm 69:9).

"But he was wounded for our transgressions, he was bruised for our iniquities: the chastisement of our peace was upon him; and with his stripes we are healed" (Isaiah 53:5).

The Words of Jesus

"The Son of man came not to be ministered unto, but to minister, and to give his life a ransom for many" (Matthew 20:28).

"The bread that I will give is my flesh, which I will give for the life of the world" (John 6:51).

The Teaching of the Apostles

"Christ died for our sins" (1 Corinthians 15:3).

"So Christ was once offered to bear the sins of many" (Hebrews 9:28).

"Christ also suffered for us . . . who his own self bare our sins in his own body on the tree" (1 Peter 2:21, 24).

"For Christ also hath once suffered, . . . the just for the unjust" (1 Peter 3:18).

When Jesus Christ died on the cross, He was taking the place of guilty sinners, willingly bearing their punishment. This was the climax to the plan of salvation God had gradually unveiled through the Old Testament rituals and ceremonies. There was the Passover, for instance, with the lamb being slain and the doorposts sprinkled with its blood. On the night before His death, Jesus celebrated the Passover with His disciples, and during that final meal together— now generally called "the Last Supper"—He took bread and wine and gave it to them, saying, "Take, eat; this is my body. . . . This is my blood of the new testament, which is shed for many for the remission of sins" (Matthew 26:26, 28). In doing that, He used the bread and wine to demonstrate that the old covenant was passing away in favor of the new, with Himself as the Lamb whose shed blood was to shield multitudes of people from the wrath of God. That is what Paul meant when he wrote that "Christ our passover is sacrificed for us" (1 Corinthians 5:7).

Then, under the old covenant, we noted the great Day of Atonement, when the priest, confessing the sins of the people, laid his hands on the head of the sacrificial animal, whose death then released the people from the penalty for their wrongdoing. In the new covenant, Jesus is "the Lamb of God, which taketh away the sin of the world" (John 1:29), and Paul says that in His death "Christ . . . hath given himself for us an offering and a sacrifice to God" (Ephesians 5:2).

There are two other important ways in which the death of Jesus confirms Old Testament teaching about the nature of God.

First, the cross reveals God's *perfect holiness and justice.* God declared that He would "by no means clear the guilty" (Exodus 34:7) and one of the prophets says of God, "Thou art of purer eyes than to behold evil, and canst not look on iniquity" (Habakkuk 1:13). God's only dealing with sin is to condemn it; He cannot regard it with anything except righteous anger. When Jesus died on the cross He was bearing in His own body the sin and guilt of multitudes. Paul says that He was made "to be sin for us" (2 Corinthians 5:21). Jesus, in His death, became truly the representative of sinners. Yet, if this is true and God is holy and righteous and cannot look upon sin, Jesus must suffer not only the physical but spiritual penalty of sin—

namely, separation from God, which is the supreme punishment for sin. Nearing the moment of physical death, Jesus cried, "My God, my God, why hast thou forsaken me?" (Matthew 27:46). No one has ever fathomed the depths of that tremendous statement, which tells of the only time when the first and second Persons of the Trinity were separated, and a holy and righteous God in heaven turned His back upon His Son on earth. Jesus Christ, God in human form, not only died physically, but also endured and exhausted the divine anger that rested on Him on account of those whose sins He bore. As Isaiah says, He was "smitten of God, and afflicted" (Isaiah 53:4). Pause for a moment and think that through! God *cannot* overlook evil. *All* sin—all *your* sin—must be punished. God is a God of absolute holiness and utter righteousness.

Second, the cross reveals God's wonderful *love.* The Old Testament revelation of God's love became even clearer in the New Testament and clearest of all at the cross. Jesus said, "God so loved the world, that he gave his only begotten Son" (John 3:16). Paul wrote, "But God demonstrates His own love toward us, in that while we were yet sinners, Christ died for us" (Romans 5:8, NASB); John added, "Hereby perceive we the love of God, because he laid down his life for us" (1 John 3:16), and "Herein is love, not that we loved God, but that he loved us, and sent his Son to be the propitiation for our sins" (1 John 4:10).

Here is the most astonishing act of love in history. Jesus Christ, the sinless Son of God, came into the world He had made, to rescue guilty, helpless sinners from the result of their sin. He was rejected by most of those who saw and heard Him. He was blasphemed, betrayed, and finally skewered to a Roman cross in an agonizing act of murder. Yet He willingly endured it all because of His overwhelming love that longed for the forgiveness of even the worst of His enemies.

Let me now ask you a simple yet serious question. What is *your* reaction to the love of God shown in the death of Jesus? Try to recall honestly the kind of person you have been. Have you been selfish? Dishonest? Impure? Proud? Envious? Greedy? Unkind? Critical? Jealous? One thing is certain—*you have not given God His rightful place in your life.* You have not loved Him with all your heart, soul, mind, and strength. Now look at Jesus dying on the cross. Think of the physical agony of those hours: His head lacerated by the crown of thorns; His back flayed by the scourge into a mass of bloody pulp; His hands and feet pinned to a rough wooden cross, so that He hung there stark naked in front of a huge crowd in the searing heat of the sun. Now add the suffering we can never begin to understand—the spiritual anguish of separation from His eternal Father, the bearing of the full weight of the penalty of sin. Hold *your sin* and *His suffering* side by side—and then remember that

Jesus suffered and died because of His overwhelming love for sinners.

Let me ask you again: what is your reaction? Do you see that you are personally involved in the cross? Paul spoke of "the Son of God, who loved me, and gave himself for me" (Galatians 2:20). Can you say that? Do the words of Charles H. Gabriel have any meaning for you?

> I stand all amazed at the love Jesus offers me,
> Confused at the grace that so freely He proffers me;
> I tremble to know that for me He was crucified—
> That for me, a sinner, He suffered, He bled, He died.
> Oh, it is wonderful that He should care for me
> Enough to die for me!
> Oh, it is wonderful, wonderful to me!

Third, the death of Jesus was victorious. The Greek philosopher Aristotle once said, "Death is a dreadful thing, for it is the end," and Sir Arthur Keith declared, "Nothing follows. Life goes out like a guttering candle." Millions have shared their hopeless beliefs, yet when we read the story of Jesus we discover that His death was *not* the end; something *did* follow. Jesus came to life again three days after He had died and been buried. The resurrection of Jesus is no mere theory, mystical belief, or spiritual theme, but a historical fact: "Christ died for our sins . . . was buried . . . rose again the third day" (1 Corinthians 15:3-4).

The evidence is overwhelming.

After Jesus had been certified as dead His body was

placed in a tomb belonging to Joseph of Arimathea. Hearing that Jesus had prophesied that He would rise again after three days, Pilate set an armed guard to prevent anyone from stealing the body and spreading rumors of resurrection. To make things doubly safe the tomb was sealed with a huge stone and secured with an official seal. It seemed that the world had seen the last of Jesus, but three days later evidence began to gather that could lead to only one conclusion— Jesus *had* risen from the dead.

The tomb was empty. Even the enemies of Jesus admitted that. The disciples could not have stolen the body without overcoming the guard, and no fight or disturbance was reported.

The dead body was never seen again. Had the authorities removed the body, they could have produced it when stories of resurrection began to circulate.

Jesus was repeatedly seen alive. He appeared on at least eleven separate occasions—to Mary Magdalene (Mark 16:9); to several women (Matthew 28:9); to two disciples (Luke 24:15); to ten disciples in an upper room (John 20:19); to eleven disciples in the same place about a week later (John 20:26); to eleven disciples in Galilee (Matthew 28:17); to the disciples on the seashore (John 21:1); to Peter (Luke 24:34); to about 500 people at once (1 Corinthians 15:6); to James (1 Corinthians 15:7); and to Paul (1 Corinthians 15:8).

The disciples were transformed. Following the crucifixion they were so bewildered that they shut themselves away "for fear of the Jews" (John 20:19). Yet soon they were preaching the resurrection everywhere, and prepared to die (as many of them did) rather than deny the truth of what they had seen with their own eyes.

Sunday was established as a day of worship. As devout Jews, the early disciples observed the Sabbath, the last day of the week; now they changed to the first day, the day Jesus rose from the dead. Only a momentous event could have brought this about after centuries of custom.

The early church flourished in Jerusalem. The Bible records that "The number of the disciples multiplied in Jerusalem greatly; and a great company of the priests were obedient to the faith" (Acts 6:7). Something quite astonishing must have happened to turn opposition and hatred into faith and love.

Many experts find the Bible's evidence beyond dispute. Here are two of many who could be quoted. Sir Edward Clarke, a British authority on Evidence, once made a prolonged study of the resurrection, and as a result he wrote, "To me, the evidence is conclusive. Over and over again in the High Court I have secured a verdict on evidence not nearly so compelling. A truthful witness is always artless and disdains effect. The Gospel evidence for the resurrection is of this class. As a lawyer I accept it unreservedly as the testimony of truthful men to facts they were able to substantiate." On April 9, 1939, Chief Justice Ben C. Hilliard, of the Colorado Supreme Court, presided when the evidence concerning the resurrection of Jesus was presented. He advised on the legal value of each piece of evidence and eventually summed up as follows: "Overwhelming evidence has been given to us tonight of the fact of the resurrection of Christ, and we must decide that Christ did rise from the dead, in deed and in truth."

Jesus Christ rose from the dead, "in deed and in truth," and as a result two important things follow.

First, His words were confirmed. In Matthew 16:21, we read: "From that time forth began Jesus to shew unto his disciples, how that he must go unto Jerusalem, and suffer many things of the elders and chief priests and scribes, and be killed, and be raised again the third day." A little later, in Matthew 20:18-19, He told His disciples: "Behold, we go up to Jerusalem; and the Son of man shall be betrayed unto the chief priests and unto the scribes, and they shall condemn him to death, and shall deliver him to the Gentiles to mock, and to scourge, and to crucify him: and the third day he shall rise again." Speaking of His body in John 2:19 He told the Jews, "Destroy this temple and in three days I will raise it up," and on several other occasions He clearly predicted His own resurrection. The fulfillment of these prophecies sets Jesus apart from ordinary men. But Jesus said that He "*must* go unto Jerusalem . . . and be killed and be raised again." Why "*must*"? Because the Old Testament had prophesied not only the birth and death of the Messiah, but also His resurrection: "For thou wilt not leave my soul in hell; neither wilt thou suffer thine Holy One to see corruption" (Psalm 16:10). Paul also linked the death and resurrection of Jesus with the Old Testament prophecies by saying that "Christ died for our sins according to the scriptures . . . he was buried, and . . . rose again the third day according to the scriptures" (1 Corinthians 15:3-4) and that "Jesus Christ our Lord . . . was . . . declared to be the Son of God with power, according to the spirit of holiness, by the resurrection from the dead" (Romans 1:3-4).

Second, His work was completed. Shortly before His death, Jesus prayed, "Father . . . I have glorified thee on the earth: I have finished the work which thou gavest me to do" (John 17:1, 4). This work included revealing to mankind something more of the nature of God, the giving of His teaching, and the training and preparation of the disciples for their tasks in the early church, but the great central work was man's salvation. This could only be done by taking man's place in separation from God, and when Jesus said "I have finished the work" He was speaking of the time when He would be nailed to the cross on behalf of sinners. When, immediately before He died, He cried out, "It is finished" (John 19:30), it was not a cry of tragedy, but of triumph. Perhaps He recalled at that moment the first covenant of grace made with man; the years of captivity in Egypt; the covenant with Moses; the giving of the Ten Commandments; the multitude of rituals and ceremonies; the thousands of animals killed in the Old Testament sacrifices; the ministries of prophets, priests, and kings; and the preaching of John the Baptist. All these had pointed to Him, and His own life on earth had pointed forward to this supreme event now taking place and prepared in God's mind "from the foundation of the world" (Revelation 13:8). This was the moment of truth, when the most stupendous work in history was being accomplished. And how do we know that it *was* accomplished? *By the resurrection!*

Let me illustrate. Years ago, England had debtors' prisons, to which men owing money were frequently sentenced. If the debtor could not be found, his guarantor could be jailed in his place. Now supposing I had contracted a debt, my guarantor had been imprisoned on my behalf, and later I saw him walking down the road a free man. I would now be sure that my debt must have been settled, because the man punished by imprisonment on my behalf was free. In a much more wonderful way, the fact that Jesus rose from the dead is proof that God's justice was satisfied by the death of His Son on behalf of sinners. The law can no longer condemn those for whom Jesus died. Paul declares that God "cancelled out the certificate

of debt consisting of decrees against us and which
was hostile to us; and He has taken it out of the way,
having nailed it to the cross" (Colossians 2:14, NASB).
The resurrection proves that Jesus has effectively accomplished the work of salvation. His death was victorious! In the very next verse Paul says that in His
death Jesus "disarmed the rulers and authorities, . . .
[and] made a public display of them, having
triumphed over them through Him" (Colossians 2:15,
NASB). It was a triumph of God's love and justice over
all the forces of evil, providing His perfect remedy for
man's guilt and sin, and the basis on which man can
get right with God.

Let us now look briefly at a few of the ways in which
the Bible describes the results of the death and resurrection of Jesus. Left to himself, man is guilty, lost,
separated from God, and utterly helpless. What hap-
pens when the death and resurrection of Christ are
applied to him?

He is justified. A man called Bildad once asked the
most baffling of questions, "How then can a man be
justified with God?" (Job 25:4). How can it ever be
possible for man to be declared not guilty by God
when he was born a sinner and is guilty of a life of sin?
Looked at the other way, how can God punish sin and
yet reverse the sentence on the sinner, declaring him
free from his guilt? Only God could provide an answer,
and He did so in the life and death of Jesus Christ

acting as man's substitute. When God declares a man righteous in His sight, He does so on the basis of the life and death of the One who was acting on his behalf. As somebody once put it,

> Because the sinless Saviour died
> My guilty soul is counted free,
> For God, the Just, is satisfied
> To look on Him, and pardon me.

That is beyond our understanding, yet is the clear teaching of the New Testament writers. Paul says, "Jesus our Lord ... was delivered for our offences, and was raised again for our justification" (Romans 4:24-25); he writes of those "justified in the name of the Lord Jesus" (1 Corinthians 6:11); and elsewhere of "the kindness and love of God our Saviour" which has resulted in men's being "justified by his grace" (Titus 3:4, 7). In explaining the meaning of *justified*, somebody once said that it was "to be just-as-if-I'd never sinned": yet it means even more than that. When a man is declared justified by God, God not only counts him as not guilty, but as righteous in His sight. The justified man is treated by God as being one with Christ, and therefore all the work of Christ belongs to him as though it were his own work. The benefits of Christ's death are his and so also are those of His life. The death of Christ deals with the penalty of all his disobedience, while Christ's righteousness—His conformity to all His Father's perfect will—is the righteousness reckoned by God to belong to each believer. In the matter of our punishment, God looks on the death of Christ and says "It is sufficient"; in the matter of our acceptance, God looks on the obedience of Christ and says "I am well pleased." As a result, the sinner is not only spared the punishment but also brought into fellowship with God. He is not only acquitted from the bar of the courtroom, but also welcomed into the heart of the family as a child of God. As Paul puts it, "Therefore being justified by faith, we have peace with God through our Lord Jesus Christ: by whom also we have access by faith into this grace wherein we stand, and rejoice in hope of the glory of God" (Romans 5:1-2).

How wonderful that is!—and all because of the amazing love of the Lord Jesus Christ to undeserving sinners.

He is redeemed. Jesus taught that He came to set men free, and when asked why this was necessary He replied, "Truly, truly, I say to you, every one who commits sin is the slave of sin" (John 8:34, NASB). Peter also spoke of men as being "slaves of corruption," adding, "for by what a man is overcome, by this he is enslaved" (2 Peter 2:19, NASB). Man is not only born a sinner; he is so gripped by sin that he cannot free himself. He is chained by his fallen nature to the selfish, godless desires of his own heart. This is the background to one of the greatest words in the Bible: *redemption*. To redeem is to set free by the payment of a price (usually described as a ransom), and this brings us to one of the most wonderful truths in the New Testament. Jesus explains His purpose in coming into the world by saying, "The Son of man came not to be ministered unto, but to minister, and to give his life a ransom for many" (Mark 10:45), and Paul underlines this again and again. He says that "God sent forth his Son, made of a woman, made under the law, to redeem them that were under the law" (Galatians 4:4-5); and that "Our Saviour Jesus Christ . . . gave himself for us, that he might redeem us from all iniquity" (Titus 2:13-14). He speaks of those who are "justified freely by his grace through the redemption that is in Christ Jesus" (Romans 3:24); he says that "Christ hath redeemed us from the curse of the law, being made a curse for us" (Galatians 3:13). He describes the Lord Jesus Christ as God's "dear Son: in whom we have redemption through his blood" (Colossians 1:13-14), and as "the beloved. In whom we have redemption through his blood" (Ephesians 1:6-7). Peter confirms this same truth, "Forasmuch as ye know that ye were not redeemed with corruptible things, as silver and gold . . . but with the precious blood of Christ, as of a lamb without blemish and without spot" (1 Peter 1:18-19).

Here is another amazing result of Christ's death. Men, born into the slavery of sin, are set free by God on the ransom payment of the blood of His Son, the Lord Jesus Christ.

He is reconciled to God. The Bible teaches that man is not only a sinner but also God's enemy. Paul writes to those who were once "enemies in your mind by wicked works" (Colossians 1:21); he looks back on his own old life and says, "we were enemies" (Romans 5:10); and teaches that "The carnal mind is enmity against God" (Romans 8:7). James writes: "Know ye not that the friendship of the world is enmity with God? whosoever therefore will be a friend of the world is the enemy of God" (James 4:4). That is one of the most serious statements in the Bible. Perhaps you ought to pause for a moment and think it over. Is this still true of you?

Now the only way in which man can be reconciled to God is by the removal of the basic cause of the enmity—his sin—and that is something he cannot do for himself. The only answer lies in the death of Christ by which sin was so effectively put away that Paul says, "Therefore being justified by faith, we have peace with God through our Lord Jesus Christ" (Romans 5:1), and a few verses later, "While we were enemies, we were reconciled to God through the death of His Son" (Romans 5:10, NASB). What a transformation! Once God's enemies, now His friends, with the cause of their enmity removed forever!

He is forgiven. Forgiveness has been called "perhaps the most glorious word in the English language." How often, when a barrier has arisen between us and someone else, we have longed to know his forgiveness. How much more does man need to know the forgiveness of God, against whom he has committed an untold number of sins? And God makes precisely this promise in the new covenant, "I will forgive their iniquity, and I will remember their sin no more" (Jeremiah 31:34). The death of Jesus formed the basis for the promise and at the Last Supper He spoke of "My blood of the covenant, which is to be shed on behalf of many for the forgiveness of sins" (Matthew 26:28, NASB).

Again the New Testament writers agree. Paul says that in Christ "We have redemption through his blood, the forgiveness of sins, according to the riches of his grace" (Ephesians 1:7), and continues, "God for Christ's sake hath forgiven you" (Ephesians 4:32). Preaching about the resurrection of Christ, he says, "Be it known unto you therefore, men and brethren, that through this man is preached unto you the forgiveness of sins" (Acts 13:38). Peter says that Jesus was raised from the dead to give "forgiveness of sins" (Acts 5:31), and John writes "Your sins are forgiven you for his name's sake" (1 John 2:12).

What a glorious experience! Man can know the complete forgiveness of his sins, because God so blots them out that they can never again be brought into reckoning. In 1874, soon after a terrible disaster had struck at the family of a Chicago lawyer, H. G. Spafford, killing four of his children in the sinking of the transatlantic steamer *Ville de Havre*, he wrote a hymn telling of his deep personal faith in God. In one of the verses he captured exactly the joy of finding complete forgiveness in the death of Christ:

> My sin—oh, the bliss of this glorious thought!
> My sin—not in part, but the whole,
> Is nailed to His cross, and I bear it no more:
> Praise the Lord, praise the Lord, O my soul!

He receives the gift of eternal life. The Bible teaches that after this life all men will face a day of judgment—"Every one of us shall give account of himself to God" (Romans 14:12). All men will pass to one of two eternal destinies. Some will be received into the conscious presence of God, with whom they will live forever without sin, sorrow, or disappointment of any kind. The Bible calls this "heaven." *All* others will be "punished with everlasting destruction from the presence of the Lord, and from the glory of his power" (2 Thessalonians 1:9), and exist forever in a condition of indescribable suffering, despair, and torment, which the Bible calls "hell." Speaking of His authority to execute this final judgment on all men, Jesus told of the day when "All that are in the graves shall hear his voice, and shall come forth; they that have done good, unto the resurrection of life; and they that have done evil, unto the resurrection of damnation" (John 5:28-29).

Yet in the death and resurrection of Jesus Christ, the possibility of hell and the terror of judgment are

removed by the gift of eternal life *here and now.*
Jesus said, "Verily, verily, I say unto you, He that heareth
my word, and believeth on him that sent me, hath
everlasting life, and shall not come into condemna-
tion; but is passed from death unto life" (John 5:24).
And again, "Verily, verily, I say unto you, He that believeth on me hath everlasting life" (John 6:47).

Speaking of this, Paul says, "The wages of sin is
death; but the gift of God is eternal life through Jesus
Christ our Lord" (Romans 6:23), and later declares
triumphantly, "There is therefore now no condemna-
tion to them which are in Christ Jesus" (Romans 8:1).
Paul knew that physical death was something "appointed unto men" (Hebrews 9:27), but the resurrection of Jesus Christ robbed death of its power. I listen
to him dismissing the darkness and fear that for so
many gathers round the grave:

> For this corruptible must put on incorruption, and
> this mortal must put on immortality. So when this
> corruptible shall have put on incorruption, and this
> mortal shall have put on immortality, then shall be
> brought to pass the saying that is written, Death is
> swallowed up in victory. O death, where is thy sting?
> O grave, where is thy victory? The sting of death is sin;
> and the strength of sin is the law. But thanks be to
> God, which giveth us the victory through our Lord
> Jesus Christ (1 Corinthians 15:53-57).

The man for whom Jesus Christ has fulfilled the
law, and for whose sins He died on the cross, fears

Right With God

neither hell, judgment, nor death, for Christ has given him the gift of eternal life. In Paul's words, "Much more then, having now been justified by His blood, we shall be saved from the wrath of God through Him" (Romans 5:9, NASB). Physical death, although still to be experienced, no longer leads to everlasting torment, but to everlasting triumph in the presence of the living God.

Here, then, in the person and work of the Lord Jesus Christ, is God's answer to man's need, the one way in which men can be justified, redeemed, reconciled to God, forgiven, and given eternal life.

5: The Need

In the life, death, and resurrection of the Lord Jesus Christ, God has provided the perfect answer to man's greatest need.

Yet not everyone has found that answer. Most men are still lost in their sin and away from God.

What is needed for God's answer to become real in a man's life and experience?

To put it personally and directly, what do *you* need in order to be right with God—to become a true Christian—to enter into God's kingdom and family? The Bible's answer comes in two statements by Jesus:

> Verily, verily, I say unto thee, Except a man be born again, he cannot see the kingdom of God (John 3:3).

> Verily I say unto you, Except ye be converted, and become as little children, ye shall not enter into the kingdom of heaven (Matthew 18:3).

Before you can "see the kingdom of God," or "enter into the kingdom of heaven," you *must* be born again, and you *must* be converted. Those are essential before you can be right with God. Let us look closely at what they mean.

You Must Be Born Again

Jesus said to a man called Nicodemus, "Ye must be born again" (John 3:7). Nicodemus had begun the conversation by praising Jesus for all the wonderful works He was doing and by acknowledging that He must surely be "a teacher come from God" (John 3:2), but Jesus went straight to the root of the matter. "Except a man be born again, he cannot see the kingdom of God." Nicodemus was baffled. "How can a man be born when he is old?" he asked. "Can he enter the second time into his mother's womb, and be born?" (verse 4). On the face of it, his misunderstanding was amazing. After all, Nicodemus was "a man of the Pharisees" (verse 1), and therefore intensely religious. The Pharisees believed in the existence of one true and holy God, and the truth of His law revealed in the Old Testament. They believed that every man was morally responsible to God and insisted on a very strict observance of hundreds of laws and traditions aimed at raising man's moral standards.

And Nicodemus was no *ordinary* Pharisee; he was "a ruler of the Jews" (verse 1), or, as Jesus put it, "a master of Israel" (verse 10). He was one of the leading religious teachers of his day and spent his life studying and teaching religion, seeking to find and follow truth and to pass it on to others. Yet he did not even begin to grasp what Jesus meant! He could not see the truth; he was spiritually blind. That is precisely the Bible's description of men who are not right with God. As Paul says, "The god of this world [the devil] has blinded the minds of the unbelieving, that they might not see the light of the gospel of the glory of Christ, who is the image of God" (2 Corinthians 4:4, NASB)—That explains why even intelligent and articulate people are baffled by the teaching of the Bible, and especially with the gospel message of the death and resurrection of Jesus Christ. They cannot see it. To some it is foolishness, to others it is a mystery, to all who are not born again it is meaningless. The "natural man does not accept the things of the Spirit of God; for they are foolishness to him, and he cannot understand them, because they are spiritually appraised" (1 Corinthians 2:14, NASB).

But this concerns *you*. If you began reading this book searching for God, you were utterly incapable of grasping even the simplest spiritual truth, because you were spiritually blind. Yet God can open your blind eyes to see spiritual truth, and nothing is more important than that you should now be asking Him to do so. Perhaps you ought to pause and pray that prayer on page 16 again, or in your own words ask God here and now to open your eyes.

Now return to John 3 and notice how Jesus answers Nicodemus's question about being born a second time: "Verily, verily, I say unto thee, Except a man be born of water and of the Spirit, he cannot enter into the kingdom of God" (verse 5). If a man is to enter the kingdom of God he needs another birth, one brought about by the Spirit, because "That which is born of the flesh is flesh; and that which is born of the Spirit is spirit" (verse 6). The word "flesh" here refers to fallen human nature, and takes us back to Adam and Eve. You will remember that their sin led to spiritual death (separation from God) and that Adam's children were then born "in his own likeness, after his image" (Genesis 5:3), so that all his descendants were born sinners by nature and as a result were sinners in practice.

Man's problem, then, lies in his birth. Born with a sinful human nature he can only act according to that nature. "That which is born of the flesh is flesh." A fallen nature cannot act spiritually; it can only produce its own likeness. Put another way, man is spiritually stillborn. He is not merely spiritually blind, without sight, but spiritually dead, without life. What can a blind man do to restore his sight? Nothing! What can a dead man do to bring life flowing into his corpse? Nothing! And no amount of self-effort will ever enable you to see or enter the kingdom of God. You were born a sinner, and, left to your own efforts, a sinner is all that you will ever be. Your trouble is too deep-rooted for you to do anything about it. Your problem lies not in your circumstances, but in your nature. Sin is not a skin complaint, but a heart disease. "That which is born of the flesh is flesh."

God's answer is put like this: "That which is born of the Spirit is spirit." The first word "Spirit" used here refers to God the Holy Spirit, and the second word "spirit" means spiritual life. God alone can bring about the spiritual birth a man needs, and when He does so His own nature is reproduced. This birth also controls the character of the life that follows. A reborn man is a new man. "That which is born of the Spirit is spirit."

This change would not take place even if a man could return to his mother's womb and be born a hundred times over. His problem would remain. A sinner's need is not *another* birth, but a *new* birth; not the *reformation* of the old life, but the *formation* of a new life—a miracle that can be performed only by God the Holy Spirit.

The Bible is so clear about this.

God's promised blessing to men in the new covenant was, "I will put My law within them, and on their heart I will write it" (Jeremiah 31:33, NASB); "I will give them one heart, and I will put a new spirit within you" (Ezekiel 11:19); "A new heart also will I give you, and a new spirit will I put within you. . . . And I will put my spirit within you" (Ezekiel 36:26-27).

The Lord Jesus Christ taught that He came to bring this new, spiritual life: "I am come that they might have life, and that they might have it more abundantly" (John 10:10); "I am the resurrection, and the life"

(John 11:25); "I am the way, the truth, and the life: no man cometh unto the Father, but by me" (John 14:6).

The apostles also taught that this new, spiritual life was essential. Paul says "For neither is circumcision (now) of any importance, nor uncircumcision, but (only) a new creation, (the result of a new birth and a new nature in Christ Jesus, the Messiah)" (Galatians 6:15, *The Amplified Bible*); and again, "And you, who were dead in trespasses and in the uncircumcision of your flesh—your sensuality, your sinful carnal nature—(God) brought to life together with (Christ)" (Colossians 2:13, *The Amplified Bible*); he says that the Christian is a person "created in Christ Jesus" (Ephesians 2:10); and that "if any man be in Christ, he is a new creature" (2 Corinthians 5:17). Finally, John writes "And this is the record, that God hath given to us eternal life, and this life is in his Son. He that hath the Son hath life; he that hath not the Son of God hath not life" (1 John 5:11-12).

That shows that the new birth is closely linked to the life, death, and resurrection of Jesus Christ, and is God's way of making real to a man what Christ did for him. When he is born again a man can speak of "the Son of God who loved me, and gave himself for me" (Galatians 2:20).

To sum up, we can say three things about the new birth. *First,* it is a mystery. No man can begin to understand it. As Jesus said to Nicodemus, "The wind blows where it wishes and you hear the sound of it, but do not know where it comes from and where it is going; so is every one who is born of the Spirit" (John 3:8, NASB). In bringing about the new birth God acts as a king, performing His own divine will as Lord of all creation, including the new creation. John says that Christians are those, "who owe their birth neither to bloods, nor to the will of the flesh (that of physical impulse), nor to the will of man (that of a natural father), but to God.—They are born of God!" (John 1:13, *The Amplified Bible*).

Second, it is a must. Jesus emphasized this to Nicodemus. "Marvel not that I said unto thee, ye must be born again." There is no alternative. The only answer to spiritual death is spiritual life. The only way to begin spiritual life is by spiritual birth. Without the new birth a man is without God, without heaven, without forgiveness, without peace, and without hope. The new birth is a must for *you*. It is the only way by which you can be brought from death to life.

Third, it is a miracle. We live in an age of amazing progress in science and technology, and this is spectacularly illustrated in the field of medicine. Surgical techniques constantly improve every year, and the transplantation of various organs of the body is now commonplace. Yet man cannot give himself a new spiritual heart and a radical and permanent transformation of his nature. That requires a miracle, which only God can perform: a man must be "born of the Spirit." Do you see the personal impact of this? For

you to be right with God will require a miracle! There is
no contribution you can make toward it, nothing you
can do to deserve it, no way in which you can control it,
no bargain you can strike in order to receive it. As Paul
says, "So then (God's gift) is not a question of human
will and human effort, but of God's mercy.—It de-
pends not on one's own willingness nor on his strenu-
ous exertion as in running a race, but on God's having
mercy on him" (Romans 9:16, *The Amplified Bible*).

All you can do is cast yourself on the mercy of God,
call upon Him, cry out to Him. Tell Him of your need,
your sin, your failure, your unbelief. Ask for His mercy.
Ask for a miracle! Christ died for sinners, so come as a
sinner. Ask Him to give you a new heart, a new birth, a
new life! And as you pray, remember God's own promise: "And ye shall seek me, and find me, when ye shall
search for me with all your heart" (Jeremiah 29:13).

You Must Be Converted

"Except ye be converted, and become as little children, ye shall not enter into the kingdom of heaven"
(Matthew 18:3).

It is important to notice the close link between the
new birth and conversion. In the new birth, God acts
independently, implanting His own divine nature into a
man's soul, and bringing that man to new life. Conversion follows the new birth, when man as a result of the
new principle of life implanted within him, obeys the
gospel with repentance and faith.

The word *converted* is widely used in everyday life. We speak of a room being converted into a workshop, a power system being converted from gas to electricity, a solid being converted into a liquid, a deficit being converted into a surplus—and we always mean a radical change. In the Bible it means turning from the old way of life to a new one. Linking this with the new birth, somebody once said that for a person to be born again was to "begin life anew in relationship to God; his manner of thinking, feeling, and acting with reference to spiritual things, undergoing a fundamental and permanent revolution." Paul reminded the Christians at Thessalonica that after they had heard the gospel they "turned to God from idols to serve the living and true God" (1 Thessalonians 1:9).

It is important to notice that they turned *from* idols and *to* God—for those are the two parts in true conversion. The first of these, turning from sin, is called repentance, and the second, turning to God, is called faith. Jesus began His public ministry by "preaching the gospel of the kingdom of God, and saying, The time is fulfilled, and the kingdom of God is at hand: *repent* ye and *believe* the gospel" (Mark 1:14-15, emphasis added). Paul also linked these two when he told the leaders of the church at Ephesus that his preaching urged "repentance toward God, and faith toward our Lord Jesus Christ" (Acts 20:21).

Before we look at them separately, let me emphasize man's responsibility in repentance and faith! They are not vague suggestions or casual invitations, but specific commands. Preaching to the people of Athens, Paul declared, God now commands "all men every where to repent," (Acts 17:30), while John says "This is his commandment, That we should believe on the name of his Son, Jesus Christ" (1 John 3:23). To be right with God, you *must* repent and you *must* have faith in the Lord Jesus Christ.

REPENTANCE

The need for repentance is surely obvious. The Bible says "All we like sheep have gone astray; we have turned every one to his own way" (Isaiah 53:6). That means that you have turned away from God, gone your own way, run your own life, made your own decisions, been your own master, and sought your own pleasure. That is why you need to repent. You are facing away from God, going the wrong direction. Unless you change direction you are chained to disaster. When told of the death of a number of Galileans in a clash with Roman soldiers, Jesus gave the warning, "Except ye repent, ye shall all likewise perish" (Luke 13:3). He went on to remind them of an accident at Siloam when 18 people were crushed to death by a falling building, adding, "Think ye that they were sinners above all men that dwelt in Jerusalem? I tell you, Nay: but, except ye repent, ye shall all likewise perish" (Luke 13:4-5). His point was obvious. These events would have reminded people that life was short and death certain—and they were not ready to die! They were not right with God. Unless they repented they would "perish," go to hell, be separated forever from the living God. *Your* need is as urgent today! God's command to repent is given in the light of the fact that "He has appointed a day, in the which he will judge the world in righteousness" (Acts 17:31). But what *is* repentance?

Repentance is not merely regret, or feeling sorry for yourself. This is often no more than self-pity or personal annoyance that some wrong action has led to inconvenience or disappointment.

Repentance is not mere resolution, or a determination to do better in the future. That can be so futile. Promising either yourself or God that you will try harder from now on is not repentance.

To repent is to turn from sin, and this involves a change of mind, a change of heart, and a change of will, and we can examine these by looking at two well-known passages. One is Psalm 51, a prayer of David, known as the psalm of repentance. The other is the story of the prodigal son in Luke 15:11-32 concerning a young man who left home with his share of his father's estate and wasted it all in a foreign country.

A change of mind. David and the prodigal son were between them guilty of envy, dishonesty, selfishness, cowardice, adultery, and murder, but eventually come the words that mark the dividing line in their lives. David says, "I acknowledge my transgressions" (Psalm 51:3), and the prodigal son says, "I have sinned" (Luke 15:18). This honest acknowledgment of personal guilt is the beginning of repentance, without which a man will get no further. Jesus said, "They that be whole need not a physician, but they that are sick" and added, "I am not come to call the righteous, but sinners to repentance" (Matthew 9:12-13). You must acknowledge your moral sickness before you can be healed, admit your sin before you can ever be forgiven, accept that you are wrong before you can ever be put right. And that is a change of mind! By nature, man is too proud to admit his guilt and a master at making excuses for his failures. He blames his background, his circumstances, his parents, his lack of education, or the failures of others. But God demands nothing less than the truth, and repentance begins by acknowledging that God is right, that you are wrong, that in His sight you are a sinner. As a young man once put it to me, "I know that I deserve to go to hell."

A change of heart. Repentance is not just acknowledging the fact of sin—it also involves sorrow *for* sin, which comes from realizing not only one's own personal uncleanness, but also the goodness and holiness of God. Notice how this is emphasized in our two passages. David cries out to God, "Against thee, thee only, have I sinned, and done this evil in thy sight" (Psalm 51:4), and the prodigal son, "Father, I have sinned against heaven, and in thy sight, and am no more worthy to be called thy son" (Luke 15:21). With both, there was deep personal sorrow, not only because of the nature of their wrongdoing, but also because they now realized the loathsomeness of their sin in God's sight. True repentance causes sorrow because a man realizes that his sin has both defiled him and defied God. Notice how Paul distinguishes between true and false sorrow for sin, "I now rejoice, not that you were made sorrowful, but that you were made sorrowful to the point of repentance; for you were made sorrowful according to the will of God. . . . For the sorrow that is according to the will of God produces a repentance without regret, leading to salvation; but the sorrow of the world produces death" (2 Corinthians 7:9-10, NASB).

Have you had that change of heart? Do you realize anything of the loathsomeness of your sin in the sight of a holy God? Do you sense anything of the terrible truth that you have not only broken His law but also grieved Him? Charles Wesley knew how vital this was to true repentance when he wrote:

> By Thy Spirit, Lord, reprove,
> All my inmost sins reveal,
> Sins against Thy light and love
> Let me see, and let me feel;
> Sins that crucified my God,
> Spilt again Thy precious blood.

A change of will. In his book *Facing Facts and*

Finding Faith, Frederick P. Wood wrote, "The will is the deciding factor in everything we do. In every sphere of life it settles alternatives." Notice this in our two passages. David prayed, "Have mercy upon me, O God. . . . Wash me thoroughly from mine iniquity, and cleanse me from my sin. Purge me with hyssop, and I shall be clean: wash me, and I shall be whiter than snow. Create in me a clean heart, O God; and renew a right spirit within me" (Psalm 51:1, 2, 7, 10). The prodigal son "arose, and came to his father" (Luke 15:20). David by his words and the prodigal son by his actions both showed a change of will. There was a true willingness, not only for the past to be forgiven, but for the future to be changed as well. This is essential. Isaiah says, "Let the wicked forsake his way, and the unrighteous man his thoughts: and let him return unto the Lord, and he will have mercy upon him; and to our God, for he will abundantly pardon" (Isaiah 55:7). Note the order! A man must forsake his sin before God will forgive it. The Bible says, "If I regard iniquity in my heart, the Lord will not hear me" (Psalm 66:18). We cannot trifle with God. He demands repentance *from* sin, not merely regret *for* it. I once spoke to two young men who asked many questions about God, religion, the Bible, and Christianity. They seemed to have many intellectual problems, but after some probing I sensed where the real barrier was and asked, "If I could give you a satisfactory answer to all the questions you have asked, would you then be willing to become Christians *if it meant changing your lives?*" "No," they replied—and that immediately revealed their real problem. They might have admitted their sin, and even felt some kind of sorrow, but they were not willing to change the direction of their lives and make God's will their supreme desire.

Are *you?* There is no escaping that question, for at this point everything hinges on your answer to it. No man can get right with God unless he is converted, no man is converted if he has not repented, and no man has truly repented unless he is willing to part with sin. Repentance is therefore both a command and a condition. Have you repented? Have you turned from your sin in real sorrow? Have you made a clean break with it? As you consider this, bear in mind that although repentance is a condition you must meet, it is also a gift of God! Although you are responsible to repent, it is a grace God bestows! Peter preached that Jesus had been raised from the dead, "to be a Prince and a Saviour, for to give repentance to Israel, and forgiveness of sins" (Acts 5:31). In the story of the conversion of Cornelius, a Roman soldier, we read, "Then hath God also to the Gentiles granted repentance unto life" (Acts 11:18). Paul told Timothy to preach the gospel faithfully and carefully even to his enemies, in the hope that God would "give them repentance to the acknowledging of the truth" (2 Timothy 2:25).

How wonderful this is! Nothing whatever need keep

you from repenting at this very moment. If you doubt whether you have ever truly repented, then ask God to help you to do so. The Bible teaches that God is "not willing that any should perish, but that all should come to repentance" (2 Peter 3:9), and nowhere is this more clearly seen than in the death of Christ on the cross, the supreme motive for you to turn from sin. "The kindness of God leads you to repentance" (Romans 2:4, NASB).

FAITH

Repentance, then, is one side of conversion. The other side is faith. We come now to the climax of all that we have seen, toward which we have been moving from the first page. Numerically, the central verse in the Bible is Psalm 118:8, which reads "It is better to trust in the Lord than to put confidence in man." Faith, or "trust in the Lord" is one of the fundamental principles of the Bible. There is no other way for a man to be right with God. The writer to the Hebrews says, "Without faith it is impossible to please him" (Hebrews 11:6). A man can come to God without great intelligence, wealth, or high social standing; he can certainly come to God without rituals and ceremonies, priest or penance; but not without faith. As Dr. W. H. Griffith Thomas put it, "Faith is our response to God's revelation; the link between God and man, and the channel of all Divine blessings."

The importance of faith is emphasized throughout

the Bible, and the various forms of the word *believe* occur over 500 times in the New Testament alone, or an average of twice in every chapter. Almost always it is centered not generally on God, but specifically on the Lord Jesus Christ as the One who "once suffered for sins, the just for the unjust, that he might bring us to God" (1 Peter 3:18). Here are some of the ways we see the importance of faith in the New Testament:

First, Jesus repeatedly said that a man must have faith if he is to be right with God: "For God so loved the world, that he gave his only begotten Son, that whosoever believeth in him should not perish, but have everlasting life" (John 3:16). "He that believeth on him is not condemned: but he that believeth not is condemned already, because he hath not believed in the name of the only begotten Son of God" (John 3:18). "He that believeth on the Son hath everlasting life: and he that believeth not the Son shall not see life; but the wrath of God abideth on him" (John 3:36).

Second, the apostles taught that faith in Christ was essential. When a jailer at Philippi asked Paul what he must do to be saved (made right with God), Paul replied "Believe on the Lord Jesus Christ, and thou shalt be saved" (Acts 16:31). Peter said that "He who believes in Him [Christ] shall not be disappointed" (1 Peter 2:6, NASB). John wrote in his gospel, "That ye might believe that Jesus is the Christ, the Son of God; and that believing ye might have life through his name" (John 20:31).

Third, all the spiritual benefits of the death and resurrection of Christ are received through faith. We looked at five of these previously: justification, redemption, reconciliation, forgiveness, and eternal life. Notice that faith is needed to receive each one of them:

Justification: Paul says, "We conclude that a man is justified by faith" (Romans 3:28).

Redemption: Paul explains that although "All have sinned, and come short of the glory of God," there are those who have been "Justified freely by his grace through the redemption that is in Christ Jesus: whom God hath set forth to be a propitiation through faith" (Romans 3:23-25).

Reconciliation: "Therefore being justified by faith, we have peace with God through our Lord Jesus Christ" (Romans 5:1).

Forgiveness: Jesus told a notoriously sinful woman, "Thy sins are forgiven. Thy faith hath saved thee" (Luke 7:48, 50).

Eternal life: Jesus said, "Verily, verily, I say unto you, He that believeth on me hath everlasting life" (John 6:47).

There is no alternative to faith, no substitute for it. Without biblical faith you remain lost in your sin. If you are to be right with God, you must turn to him in faith. Have you done so? Do you "believe on the Lord Jesus Christ?" Your search for God will never end unless you come to this point. Jesus said, "I am the way, the truth, and the life: no man cometh unto the Father, but by me" (John 14:6), and the Holy Spirit inspired Peter, speaking of the risen Christ, to say, "There is none other name under heaven given among men, whereby we must be saved" (Acts 4:12).

This leads us to an all-important question: What *is* faith?

I want to answer that question from the Bible as simply and helpfully as I can, so that it might be applied to you in a vital, personal way. As with repentance, mind, heart, and will are all involved.

Faith concerns *the mind.* The Bible calls faith "the assurance of things hoped for, the conviction of things not seen" (Hebrews 11:1, NASB) It is being sure of things we cannot see. In the same chapter we read, "For he who comes to God must believe that He is and that He is a rewarder of those who seek Him" (Hebrews 11:6, NASB), and this clarifies the truth. If you are to come to God, you must believe that there *is* a God. If you are to believe *on* the Lord Jesus Christ, you must first believe *in* Him; not only in the facts of His life, death, and resurrection, but in the truth of His claim to be God and in the value of His work. When the Pharisees challenged His claim to be God, Jesus answered: "If ye believe not that I am he, ye shall die in your sins" (John 8:24). Again, if you are to come as a sinner, you must believe that you *are* a sinner, or there would be no sense in your coming.

These truths about the character of God, the person and work of Christ, and your own personal condition are found in the Bible, and that is why Paul says that "Faith cometh by hearing, and hearing by the word of God" (Romans 10:17). Yet many read the Bible without believing it to be either true or relevant. Why? The Bible's answer is that God alone, by the Holy Spirit, can cause men to see the truth of His Word. Faith, even in this sense, is a gift of God. Do you believe in the God who reveals Himself in the Bible? Do you believe that Jesus is "the Christ, the Son of the living God" (Matthew 16:16)? Do you believe that He died for sinners on the cross and rose from the dead on the third day? Do you believe that you are a guilty sinner in the sight of God? Then you have the beginning of faith!

Faith concerns *the heart.* When the Bible speaks of the heart, it does not mean the physical organ that pumps blood around the body, but rather the center of man's emotions, desires, and affections. With the mind, man becomes informed; with the heart man becomes involved. And when the Bible talks about faith it means getting involved!

Believing in the facts obviously is not enough, and there are several striking examples of this in the New Testament. Acts 8 records the story of a magician called Simon who, when he heard the gospel, believed (verse 13), was baptized, and followed Philip, who was preaching in Samaria at the time; but later it became obvious that he was not really converted, because Peter told him that he was still "in the gall of bitterness, and in the bond of iniquity" (verse 23). James writes, "You believe that God is one. You do well; the demons also believe, and shudder" (James 2:19, NASB). This truth was illustrated several times in the course of Jesus' public ministry, when evil spirits openly acknowledged Him to be "Jesus, thou Son of God" (Matthew 8:29); "the Holy One of God" (Mark 1:24); "the Son of God" (Mark 3:11); and "Christ the Son of God" (Luke 4:41). In Acts 26, when Paul told King Agrippa of his conversion, and had spoken of Christ as the promised Messiah, he asked, "King Agrippa, do you believe the Prophets? I know that you do" (verse 27, NASB). The king's reply was brief, angry, and scornful, "In a short time you will persuade me to become a Christian!" (verse 28, NASB). Agrippa believed, but was not a Christian.

Faith concerns the heart as well as the mind, as the truth grips a man in a personal way. The Bible says that "With the heart man believeth unto righteousness" (Romans 10:10), and without this deep personal involvement, there is no saving faith. Here faith becomes intensely personal, and not just abstract knowledge of the truth. Paul did not speak about the death of Christ in a cold, detached way, but cried "I have been crucified with Christ; and it is no longer I who live, but Christ lives in me; and the life which I now live in the flesh I live by faith in the Son of God, who loved me and delivered himself up for me" (Galatians 2:20, NASB).

This is wonderfully illustrated by the conversion of John Wesley. Born into a very religious family, he went to Oxford University, and later became a Church of England minister, preaching throughout Great Britain and in America. He was a brilliant scholar, had great knowledge of the Bible, and at Oxford had been the leader of the Holy Club, yet when he went back from America in 1738 he wrote: "It is now two years and almost four months since I left my native country, in order to teach the Georgian Indians the nature of Christianity. But what have I learned myself in the meantime? Why, what I least of all suspected, that I, who went to America to convert others, was never myself converted to God." He became increasingly unsure and unsettled. On May 24, 1738, he went to a service held in a small building in Aldersgate Street. During the service a man began to read comments made by Martin Luther on the epistle to the Romans. Suddenly, the truth gripped John Wesley's heart. This is how he described it: "About a quarter before nine, while he was describing the change which God works in the heart through faith in Christ, I felt my heart strangely warmed. I felt I did trust in Christ, Christ alone for my salvation; and an assurance was given me that He had taken away *my* sins, even *mine*, and saved *me* from the law of sin and death."

Has your heart been gripped like that? Do you

sense the *personal* truth of what happened when Christ died on the cross? Can you say that in spite of all your sin Christ died for *you*? Even if there has not been as dramatic a moment as that experienced by John Wesley, does the same truth *now* grip *you*?

Faith concerns *the will.* In daily life, to have faith in a person is to have confidence in him, to believe that he is trustworthy; but in the Bible faith has a deeper meaning. Here are some of the ways in which it has been described:

> Faith rests on a person. Faith is that act by which one person, a sinner, commits himself to another Person, a Saviour.
>
> It is the attitude of complete trust in Christ, of reliance on Him alone for all that salvation means.
>
> What is it to believe on Christ? It is to feel your need of Him, to believe that He is able and willing to save you now, and to cast yourself unreservedly upon His mercy, and trust in Him alone for salvation.

These ideas confirm the Bible's teaching that faith is an act of personal commitment, and not merely a combination of knowledge and feelings. Jesus says "He that believeth on him is not condemned" (John 3:18); "He that believeth on the Son hath everlasting life" (John 3:36); "Whosoever believeth on me should not abide in darkness" (John 12:46). John describes the children of God as those who "believe on his name" (John 1:12); and, as we saw earlier, Paul's answer to the question "What must I do to be saved?"

was, "Believe on the Lord Jesus Christ, and thou shalt be saved" (Acts 16:31).

But remember, too, that faith goes hand in hand with repentance. Conversion is both turning *from* and turning *to*. There is no faith without repentance, and no repentance without faith. To get right with God means renouncing sin and relying on Christ.

Have you ever taken that step? Are you prepared to take it? Are you prepared to take it now? In God's name, I ask you to do so—in the light of God's sovereignty; in the light of His holiness; in the light of His law; in the light of your sin; in the light of your guilt; in the light of God's love; in the light of Christ's death and resurrection; in the light of the certainty of death and judgment; in the light of heaven and hell; and in the light of God's clear command.

Early in the 19th Century, Charlotte Elliott came to realize that in spite of all her sincere respectability she was out of touch with God. For a long time she wrestled with the problem, until at last she realized her need, which was to come to Christ in repentance and faith and to trust Him as her personal Savior. After her conversion she put her experience into words that have since become one of the world's best-known hymns and have helped many people all over the world to make their own commitments to Christ. This is not surprising, for they speak so clearly of man's sin, guilt, and helplessness before God, of the futility of his own efforts, of the Lord Jesus Christ as the Lamb of

God who alone can take away sin, and of the wonderful love of God that draws men to Himself. Here are the
words Charlotte Elliott wrote to describe the end of her
search for God:

> Just as I am, without one plea
> But that Thy blood was shed for me,
> And that Thou bidd'st me come to Thee,
> O Lamb of God, I come.
>
> Just as I am, and waiting not
> To rid my soul of one dark blot;
> To Thee whose blood can cleanse each spot,
> O Lamb of God, I come.
>
> Just as I am, though tossed about
> With many a conflict, many a doubt;
> Fightings within, and fears without,
> O Lamb of God, I come.
>
> Just as I am, poor, wretched, blind;
> Sight, riches, healing of the mind,
> Yea, all I need, in Thee to find,
> O Lamb of God, I come.
>
> Just as I am, Thou wilt receive,
> Wilt welcome, pardon, cleanse, relieve;
> Because Thy promise I believe,
> O Lamb of God, I come.
>
> Just as I am, Thy love unknown
> Has broken every barrier down;
> Now, to be Thine, yea, Thine alone,
> O Lamb of God, I come.

You will notice that every verse ends with the words *I come*. For Charlotte Elliott they were more than poetry—they were *real*. They expressed her wholehearted response to the love of God, her genuine, personal commitment to Christ.

Are they real to *you*? Do you sense that they *should* be? Then repent of your sin and turn in faith to Christ. Trust in Him. Commit yourself to Him. Cast yourself upon Him, upon His mercy, His love, His grace, His willingness to save even the worst of sinners.

The words of Charlotte Elliott's hymn could be the very words of your prayer as you come, while these prayers from the pages of the Bible express the same response:

> Return, O Lord, deliver my soul: oh save me for thy mercies' sake (Psalm 6:4).
>
> Hear, O Lord, when I cry with my voice: have mercy also upon me, and answer me (Psalm 27:7).
>
> Have mercy upon me, O God, according to thy lovingkindness: according unto the multitude of they tender mercies blot out my transgressions. Wash me throughly from mine iniquity, and cleanse me from my sin (Psalm 51:1-2).
>
> Heal me, O Lord, and I shall be healed; save me and I shall be saved: for thou art my praise (Jeremiah 17:14).
>
> God be merciful to me a sinner (Luke 18:13).

Let nothing whatever keep you back from turning to Christ here and now, immediately, wholeheartedly, even as you read this page. God commands you to do so and invites you to do so, but remember that He also warns against the danger of delay:

Do not boast about tomorrow, for you do not know what a day may bring forth (Proverbs 27:1, NASB).

Seek ye the Lord while he may be found, call ye upon him while he is near (Isaiah 55:6).

Behold, now is the accepted time; behold now is the day of salvation (2 Corinthians 6:2).

To day if ye will hear his voice, harden not your hearts (Hebrews 3:7-8).

Finally, remember the wonderful promises God makes to all who truly turn to Him in repentance and faith:

Let the wicked forsake his way, and the unrighteous man his thoughts: and let him return unto the Lord, and he will have mercy upon him; and to our God, for he will abundantly pardon (Isaiah 55:7).

And ye shall seek me, and find me, when ye shall search for me with all your heart (Jeremiah 29:13).

All that the Father giveth me shall come to me; and him that cometh to me I will in no wise cast out (John 6:37).

Verily, verily, I say unto you, He that believeth on me hath everlasting life (John 6:47).

If you come to Christ in the spirit of these prayers, in the light of these warnings, and on the basis of these promises, your search will be over.

You will be right with God.

6: The Way Ahead

The Bible describes a born-again person as being "in Christ," and goes on to say, "Therefore, if any man is in Christ, he is a new creature; the old things passed away; behold, new things have come" (2 Corinthians 5:17, NASB). This experience was so vivid to David that he said, The Lord "hath put a new song in my mouth, even praise unto our God" (Psalm 40:3). Centuries later Billy Bray, a Cornish preacher, said of his conversion, "I remember this, that everything looked new to me—the fields, the cattle, the trees. I was like a new man in a new world."

Although the intensity of feelings may not be the same for everyone, the same fact remains: a Christian is a new person; he has begun a new life, with new interests, new ambitions, new standards, a new sense of security, and a new strength in facing life's problems and demands.

Before Paul's conversion he violently persecuted those who were Christians, and he once received permission from the religious authorities to go to

Damascus "so that if he found any belonging to the Way, both men and women, he might bring them bound to Jerusalem" (Acts 9:2, NASB). "The Way" referred, of course, to Christianity, and is one of the Bible's descriptions of the Christian life. Isaiah calls it "the way of holiness" (Isaiah 35:8); David, "the way of the righteous" (Psalm 1:6); Luke, "the way of God" (Acts 18:26); Paul, "the way of peace" (Romans 3:17); and Peter, "the right way" (2 Peter 2:15). You will remember that the Bible says of unconverted people, "We have turned every one to his own way" (Isaiah 53:6). In becoming a Christian you have turned from going your own sinful, self-centered way, and are now ready to start moving in the direction of God's will. In this last chapter I want to tell you three things about "the Way" you have now begun.

It Is a Way of Openness

God's instructions to the Israelites about worship included the construction of a Tabernacle, a portable building for worship during their years of wandering in the wilderness. The most important part of this building was called the Holy of Holies, or the Holiest, in which was kept the ark of the Covenant, a gold-covered chest containing the Ten Commandments and symbolizing God's presence with His people. Only the high priest was allowed to enter the Holy of Holies, and then only once a year, on the great Day of Atonement, when he took with him blood from the sacrificial animal and sprinkled it there, making atonement for the priests and people. When the people finally settled in the land of Canaan, the temporary Tabernacle was replaced by a permanent Temple. It also had a Holy of Holies, shut off from the rest of the building by a huge veil or curtain, a symbol that no ordinary man could ever approach God.

This will help you to understand something very important that happened on the day Jesus was crucified. We read that at the moment of His death "The veil of the temple was torn in two from top to bottom" (Matthew 27:51, NASB). In this way, God dramatically demonstrated that the old covenant was now replaced by the new. The old rituals and ceremonies were now finished. The Lamb of God, the Lord Jesus Christ, had been slain once for all, and every believer now had access to God. The writer of the letter to the Hebrews clarified this when he said: "Having therefore, brethren, boldness to enter into the holiest by the blood of Jesus, by a new and living way which he hath consecrated for us, through the veil, that is to say, his flesh; and having an high priest over the house of God; let us draw near with a true heart in full assurance of faith" (Hebrews 10:19-22). The torn veil in the Temple symbolized the body of Jesus, which was torn on the cross at that very moment, His shed blood establishing the new covenant under which all Christians now have "a new and living way" into the presence of God.

Do you see how wonderful this is for *you*? Under the old covenant, only the high priest could approach God. Now every Christian can. The priest had to offer a new sacrifice every time he came, but Jesus "offered one sacrifice for sins for all time" (Hebrews 10:12, NASB). The priest entered the Holy of Holies one day a year—but the Christian can come to God every day. All the barriers have been torn down. As a Christian you have full and continuous access to God because of Christ's death on your behalf.

The way to use this access is by prayer; and this is so vital in the Christian life.

In prayer you are able to *worship* God; to praise Him for His power, His holiness, His majesty, His glory. David says, "O magnify the Lord with me, and let us exalt his name together" (Psalm 34:3).

You will be able to *thank* Him for all His goodness and love to you, for all the daily gifts of food, health, fresh air, ability of mind and body, and all that makes life worthwhile. Above all you will want to thank Him for "his unspeakable gift" (2 Corinthians 9:15), the Lord Jesus Christ, who gave His life for you on the cross. The Bible says "It is a good thing to give thanks unto the Lord, and to sing praises unto thy name, O most High" (Psalm 92:1), and that as Christians we should "In every thing give thanks: for this is the will of God Christ Jesus concerning you" (1 Thessalonians 5:18).

Then, in prayer, you will be able to *confess* your sins to God. The Christian, while eternally secure in God's keeping, is not perfect, and although God will enable you to make real progress in overcoming temptation, you will still commit sin. John taught this, and also pointed to the remedy, "If we say that we have no sin, we deceive ourselves, and the truth is not in us. If we confess our sins, he is faithful and just to forgive us our sins, and to cleanse us from all unrighteousness" (1 John 1:8-9). When you realize that you have sinned, confess it to God, and rely on His promise to forgive you.

Finally, in prayer you can *ask* God for His blessing upon you and others, for strength, guidance, wisdom, faithfulness, for His daily help in all the problems of life. The Christian should pray "for all men" (1 Timothy 2:1), for the leaders of the nations, for Christian leaders, preachers and missionaries, for those who are suffering in mind or body, for those who mourn, for those who are unconverted, for the members of his own family. The list is endless, but the command is clear, "Be careful for nothing; but in every thing by prayer and supplication with thanksgiving let your requests be made known unto God" (Philippians 4:6). As you grow in the Christian life and learn more and more to pray for the right things in the right way, you will discover the truth of the promise which Jesus made, "If ye abide in me, and my words abide in you, ye shall ask what ye will, and it shall be done unto you" (John 15:7).

Yet prayer is not mechanical. When you were born

again you became a child of God. The Bible says, "For ye are all the children of God by faith in Christ Jesus" (Galatians 3:26). In prayer you speak to your Father! That does not mean that you come *casually* to God in prayer, but you can come *confidently*, sure that God loves you and intends to bless you. Learn to come to God on that basis! The Christian life is a way of openness.

It Is a Way of Obedience

When Peter and the other apostles were questioned about their activities by the Jewish authorities, they replied "We ought to obey God rather than men" (Acts 5:29). The word "ought" means "owe it," and explains why the Christian should seek to live a life of obedience to God—he owes it to God to do so. He owes it to God as his Creator, he owes it to Him as the One who supplies his every need, and above all he owes it to Him as his Savior and Redeemer. Paul linked the Christian's obedience with the death of Christ as his Savior in this way: "For to this end Christ both died, and rose, and revived, that he might be Lord both of the dead and living" (Romans 14:9). Again, writing to the Christians at Corinth, he said that those for whom Christ died "should not henceforth live unto themselves, but unto him which died for them, and rose again" (2 Corinthians 5:15).

During the last year of his life the great missionary Spencer Walton wrote in his diary, "The will of God:

nothing less, nothing more, nothing else." What a fine motto for your entire Christian life! Make that your aim, and you will experience the truth of God's promise, "No good thing will he withhold from them that walk uprightly" (Psalm 84:11).

It is in the Bible that you will find the directions, warnings, promises, and commandments you will need to make progress in the Christian life. You must therefore give time to the careful reading and studying of the Bible, to memorizing its truth and meditating on its value. From the very beginning of your Christian life build the habit of reading the Bible regularly, daily. Set aside a time—first thing in the morning has proved best for most people—when you can get quietly alone to read the Bible and pray. Because it is the Word of God, come to your Bible eagerly, humbly, gratefully, reverently, hungrily. Above all, come to it dependently. Remember that only the Holy Spirit can really explain its meaning and apply it to your heart and life, so whenever you turn to the Bible make sure that you specifically ask for His help. Remember, too, that Bible reading is not an end in itself. James urges us to be "doers of the word, and not hearers only, deceiving your own selves" (James 1:22). It is not enough merely to read the Bible for information. Your aim should be to "grow in grace, and in the knowledge of our Lord and Saviour Jesus Christ" (2 Peter 3:18). The Christian life is a way of obedience!

It Is a Way of Opportunity

In many spheres of life, progress is best made by those who make the most of their opportunities, and that is certainly true in spiritual things. The unconverted person is in the terrible position that he "cannot please God" (Romans 8:8). However hard he tries, his life will never be pleasing to God, satisfying to himself, or of eternal worth to others. That was once true of you, but becoming a Christian has reversed your condition, opening many wonderful doors of opportunity for you. Be sure that you make the most of them. Of the many that could be mentioned, here are three.

First, you have the opportunity of bringing glory to God. One of the most exciting things about being a Christian is that every day is an opportunity to please God, to bring glory to His name, to demonstrate His power to change lives. That is because at your new birth the Holy Spirit came to dwell within you, and His concern is to direct you into the will of God and enable you to do it. It should therefore be the dominating concern of your life. Jesus said, "Seek ye first the kingdom of God, and his righteousness" (Matthew 6:33); and Paul added, "Whatsoever ye do, do all to the glory of God" (1 Corinthians 10:31). Nothing is more wonderful about the Christian life than that every day, regardless of its problems and pressures, its trials and temptations, its dangers and difficulties, is an opportunity to "Let your light so shine before men, that they may see your good works, and glorify your Father which is in heaven" (Matthew 5:16).

Second, you have the opportunity of Christian fellowship. In becoming a Christian you have not only gained a Father but a family, for every other Christian in the world is now your brother or sister in Christ. This family of Christians is called the church. In the Bible the word *church* never refers to a building, but always to people, to Christians. A family functions properly when the members meet and grow together, so God's will for His children is that they should meet together in fellowship. This word *fellowship* means "sharing," and helps us to understand the value of coming together as Christians. We are able to share our problems, our knowledge, our gifts, our faith, and above all our own personal experience of Jesus Christ as Savior and Lord. Some are leaders, all are learners, and together we grow in knowledge and holiness.

It is therefore very important that you join a local church if you do not already belong to one. Of course not everybody who attends church is a Christian—perhaps this was true of you when you picked up this book—and I am afraid it is also true that some churches have strayed a long way from the Bible's teaching about itself, the nature of God, the nature of man, sin, the person and work of Christ, the new birth, repentance, faith, and holiness. So try to find a church that is soundly based on God's Word, and join yourself to it. As Jesus regularly attended His own local place of worship, His followers should do the same, "not for-saking our own assembling together, as is the habit of some, but encouraging one another" (Hebrews 10:25. NASB).

Third, you have the opportunity of Christian ser-vice. I once heard a Dutch journalist tell of his conver-sion and early days as a Christian. Slowly he realized that his gift as a writer could be of value in God's service, and one day he placed his pen on the table and said to God "Here is my pen: if You can use it, it's Yours!" These words were not used irreverently, but simply expressed the honest desire of a new Christian. Every Christian should have the same attitude, one of willingness for God to use him in His service. Al-though we are not saved *by* good works, the Bible makes it clear that as Christians we are "created in Christ Jesus for good works, which God prepared beforehand, that we should walk in them" (Ephesians 2:10, NASB). Paul calls himself "a servant of Jesus Christ" (Romans 1:1) and says that at our conversion we are "made free from sin, and become servants to God" (Romans 6:22).

God may or may not call you to be a full-time missionary or minister, but what is certain is that He has a specific work for *you*. Begin to ask Him what it is, and "Whatsoever he saith unto you, do it" (John 2:5). Your local church will be an obvious outlet for the gifts God has given you, and you should share in its Chris-tian service, perhaps among young people, children, old folk, immigrants, or some other group in which you have a special interest. Then there are your own personal circumstances at home, school, or work. You are probably surrounded by people who are without God and may never have heard the gospel clearly. Take the God-given opportunity of sharing with them the wonderful truth of your own experience. Do it courteously and thoughtfully. It may be helpful to pass on some good Christian literature to them, or to invite them to a Christian meeting. Jesus told His disciples, "ye shall be witnesses unto me" (Acts 1:8), and we have the same privilege and opportunity today. But remember that what you *are* will count just as much as what you *say*, and your immediate opportunity for Christian service is the one to live in such a way "that the name of our Lord Jesus Christ may be glorified in you, and ye in him" (2 Thessalonians 1:12). The Christian life is a way of opportunity!

As you close this book and move on into these first days of your life as a Christian, my prayer for you is in the words of the writer of the epistle to the Hebrews 2,000 years ago. May God answer it in your life!

> Now the God of peace, that brought again from the dead our Lord Jesus, that great shepherd of the sheep, through the blood of the everlasting covenant, make you perfect in every good work to do his will, working in you that which is wellpleasing in his sight, through Jesus Christ; to whom be glory for ever and ever. Amen (Hebrews 13:20-21).

Moody Press, a ministry of the Moody Bible Institute, is designed for education, evangelization, and edification. If we may assist you in knowing more about Christ and the Christian life, please write us without obligation: Moody Press, c/o MLM, Chicago, Illinois 60610.